THE
WONDERING
YEARS

THE
WONDERING
YEARS

HOW POP CULTURE
HELPED ME ANSWER LIFE'S
BIGGEST QUESTIONS

Knox McCoy

W PUBLISHING GROUP

AN IMPRINT OF THOMAS NELSON

Published in Nashville, Tennessee, by W Publishing, an imprint of Thomas Nelson.

Author is represented by the literary agency of Alive Communications, Inc., 7680 Goddard Street, Suite 200, Colorado Springs, CO 80920, www.alivecommunications.com.

Thomas Nelson titles may be purchased in bulk for educational, business, fund-raising, or sales promotional use. For information, please e-mail SpecialMarkets@ThomasNelson.com.

Scripture quotations are taken from the Holy Bible, New International Version®, NIV®. Copyright © 1973, 1978, 1984, 2011 by Biblica, Inc.® Used by permission of Zondervan. All rights reserved worldwide. www.zondervan. com. The "NIV" and "New International Version" are trademarks registered in the United States Patent and Trademark Office by Biblica, Inc.®

Any Internet addresses, phone numbers, or company or product information printed in this book are offered as a resource and are not intended in any way to be or to imply an endorsement by Thomas Nelson, nor does Thomas Nelson vouch for the existence, content, or services of these sites, phone numbers, companies, or products beyond the life of this book.

ISBN 978-0-7852-2091-6 (eBook)
ISBN 978-0-7852-2084-8 (TP)

Library of Congress Cataloging-in-Publication Data
Library of Congress Control Number: 2018907011

Printed in the United States of America
18 19 20 21 22   LSC   10 9 8 7 6 5 4 3 2 1

For Rowe, Sidda Gray, and Marlowe. In all the fictional worlds I've visited, the one I share here with you is my most favorite.

Contents

On Introductions

I gotta say, as a society we have really lost our way when it comes to introductions. It's all lede-burying and the transfer of nonessential information.

A typical introduction goes something like, "Hello, I'm Duane. I work in IT." Think about that. What do we know about Duane now? Basically his name and his job, two things that 92 percent of Americans report being dissatisfied with.[1]

And I'm going to admit to you that I have no idea what IT even means. Something about technology or computers, probably. Intrepid Technploger? Illuminati Taskforce? I dunno. Sure, I could google it and find out, but that would take effort and I just don't care that much. Which is the essence of modern-day introductions: no one cares that much.

You know who does introductions right? People on *Game of Thrones*. Specifically the show's central figure, Daenerys Targaryen. Listen to the impression she makes with her title: *Daenerys Stormborn of the House Targaryen, First of Her Name, the Unburnt,*

---

1. Not a real stat. But it *feels* like a real stat, no?

Queen of the Andals and the First Men, Khaleesi of the Great Grass Sea, Breaker of Chains, and Mother of Dragons.

That is such a satisfying introduction it should probably come with a cigarette. We get a lot of stuff we can figure out (example: she probably can't be burnt, I'm assuming?) as well as some stuff we need more info on ("So, Daenerys, tell me more about these dragons you mother. What's their thing? What are they about?")

Bottom line: It's a great introduction because it entertains, informs, and gives tons of material regarding who she is and what she's about. Quite a bit better than "Duane from IT," right?

Let's look at another great introduction: the theme song of *The Fresh Prince of Bel-Air.* It is sonically pleasing *and* it provides the foundational context of the show. In the span of a couple of minutes, we get the following info:

- Will grew up and came to physical maturity in West Philadelphia.
- There, he was often found spending his days on the playground.
- This was the setting for one skirmish with such ominous forebodings that his mother feared for Will's safety.
- Therefore, she put him in a taxicab and sent him from Philadelphia to Bel-Air.[2]

That's an entire origin story delivered concisely, delightfully, and expertly by the lead character. It only makes sense that you'd want to watch the episode to follow.

One last example of introductions done well: *The Lion King.* As far as I'm concerned, it's the pièce de résistance of introductions.

---

2. Does it matter that the cab ride would have meant Will rode approximately 2,750 miles? It's called suspension of disbelief, you guys.

We're introduced to the setting of Pride Rock with a broad lyrical rumination of how we are all very much connected, through an Elton John song, which, I think we can all agree, is the most obvious vehicle for a rumination like that.

And the central message of this lyrical sequence is thematically crucial. It's important that the viewer buy into this idea of connection and how circular the circle of life is, because all the animals in the movie already fully embrace this idea.

As the movie begins, we're introduced to all the animals traveling to Pride Rock where their lion king, Mufasa, lives with his royal family. Everyone is really feeling the celebratory vibe, and Rafiki, the shaman-monkey character, walks through the crowd and bear-hugs (monkey-hugs?) Mufasa like they are BFFs, despite probably not being naturally simpatico in the wild. I can't authoritatively say that monkeys and lions are adversaries in the wild, but if I had to guess, I would say that they probably aren't allies—final answer, Regis. But, because of Elton's song, we remember the circle of life thing, so it's fine. We go with it.

Next we realize the animals are celebrating the birth of Mufasa's son, Simba, the future king of Pride Rock. Here's where things get crazy: Rafiki presents Simba to the gathered animals and they *lose it*. These animals are for real acting like Oprah just gave them a car.

The monkeys act like they've freebased illegal stimulants, the antelopes are going bonkers supreme, and the giraffes literally *cannot even* with all of this lion-cub cuteness. These animals are handling this situation like white people would handle a 75-percent-off sale at Pottery Barn.[3]

---

3. I say *would handle* because Pottery Barn never offers any kind of significant discount. They just make you stare down the reality that like it or not, you will pay $129 for a table runner and there's nothing you can do about it.

We can all agree that this atmosphere is a little incredible, right? Rafiki is honoring the apex predator that feeds on all these animals (Mufasa) by presenting the next apex-predator legacy monster (Simba) who will not only feed on some of the very animals that are present, but also, probably, the children and grandchildren of those animals.

Imagine knowing that your current boss's son, no matter what, will eventually lord over you just because of "the circle of employment." Could you conjure up that kind of enthusiasm for your boss's son? I'm telling you right now that I super could not.

Anyway, the best part about this opening sequence is that, straight out of the gate, we get a sense of the royal hierarchy, the central players, and the primary character, Simba. Rafiki literally holds him up as a light shines on him.

Wouldn't life be better if all stories followed this template? You wouldn't have to trouble yourself with whether or not Duane from IT is someone you should spend time getting to know.

My point is, the best introductions tell you what is up concisely *and* creatively. You get a little bit of information with a side of entertainment. And truthfully, I just want a proper introduction and context on who I'm spending time with. Ever notice how some books jump right into things like we've been dropped into a noir crime novel?

"Gutshot and panicked, I arrived at the destination of my emotional abyss."

An opening line like this and I'm like, "Who is this gutshot person? And what abyss destination have we arrived at? Is it a Chuck E. Cheese? Or a *metaphorical* Chuck E. Cheese?"

Maybe I'm a simple man with simple desires, but I like to get to know someone before arriving at the destination of our emotional abysses together, you know what I mean?

For example, if we were meeting, I'd want to communicate the following in an effort to make a connection with you:

I am Knox, December-born, of the House McCoy, First of His Name Probably, Easily Burnt on Beaches, King of the Grill and the Barbecue Smoker and Allergic to Grass, Cats, and Shellfish, Breaker of Small Talk and Social Engagements at the Last Minute If at All Possible, and Father of Poorly Conceived Yet Ambitious Metaphors.

And now that we have that connection, you should probably also know that everything I know about life I learned in some part from *The Wonder Years*.

The theme song—Joe Cocker's cover of "With a Little Help from My Friends"—taught me the need for community.

The use of adult Kevin as younger Kevin's narrator made me aware that there might be an omniscient presence observing my life too. (Definitely God, but sometimes Santa too, and they probably compared notes.)

And remember how for a hot minute, everyone thought Josh Saviano, the actor who played Kevin's best friend Paul, grew up to be Marilyn Manson? That made me confront a reality in which the world of popular culture could fold neatly into the realm of spirituality and potential principalities of darkness.

As a kid, I spent a lot of time caught up in my own thoughts and chasing them around inside my head. I spent time parsing silly things like why Donkey Kong was called "donkey" when he was really a giant ape or how on earth Kevin Arnold could snag Winnie Cooper.

But I also tried deconstructing deeper questions, like who God was and what it was that he wanted from me. It was often pop culture that helped me fill in the gaps of my understanding—sometimes in hilarious ways, and sometimes in ways that were accidentally profound.

And that's what this book is about: how I navigated life in the time I call *the wondering years.*

one

The First Time I Was Punched in the Face

The first time I got punched in the face was when I was ten years old, and it was by this real jerkface named Daniel. I don't know if that's the median age for face punching among white American kids, but that was when my number came up. Up to this point, my only experience with punching came from Mike Tyson's *Punch-Out!!* on Nintendo[1] and action movies, most notably the *Rocky* movies.

You may not be familiar with Sylvester Stallone's *Rocky* franchise. In a nutshell, Rocky Balboa was a boxer from Philly who could definitely throw a punch, but his thing was that he could take a punch. Multiple punches. *All* the punches, even. In the first movie, Rocky fought the heavyweight world champ, Apollo Creed, to a split decision simply because he was preeminently punchable. Like Johnny Depp gains strength from playing weird characters or Taylor Swift grows more powerful from relationship complications,

---

1. Fun fact: I never made it past Piston Honda, as the directness of the conflict via my Nintendo gave me too much anxiety. This foreshadowed my future fighting abilities.

so too did Rocky gain strength from getting punched. As such, I assumed this would be the same for me.[2]

To be completely honest, I should have seen it coming. Daniel and I went to school together, though we were never in the same class. He had been held back a year in school, as is often the way with bullies.[3] Our rivalry was essentially about athletics, and this came into full focus on Field Day, which is basically Elementary School Olympics.[4]

Anyway, on a random day in the fall, I was hanging out at my best friend Blake's house, and Daniel, who lived nearby, came over. This wasn't out of the ordinary; I was often over at Blake's house and I regularly crossed paths with Daniel. Despite a healthy subtext of dislike between the two of us, Daniel and I still played together because, frankly, it would have been weird not to.

I'm convinced this is where kids and adults diverge; if kids don't like each other, they just deal with it because they don't have any recourse and their world isn't that big yet. For adults though, the sky is the limit. You can turn mutual friends against that person, subtweet them via social media, or ignore them in the detergent aisle at Publix. But kids, man, they just deal.

---

2. Narrator voice: *It was very much not the same for me.*

3. Just once, I'd love to see a precocious kid who skipped a grade or two be the chief antagonist of much older and more physically mature kids. Not that I advocate kid-on-kid violence, but it would be a change of pace, right? Imagine any of the kids from *Stranger Things* bullying someone like Biff Tannen from *Back to the Future*. You can't pretend you aren't at least a little interested in that movie.

4. Field Day was the only day of school that really mattered to me. When we received our class assignments at the end of summer, the only thing I was interested in was how many athletes the classroom assignment gods had gifted to me. I didn't care so much about having my friends in class with me or whether I got the teacher who yelled a lot. I just wanted to be part of a classroom roster filled with that sweet, premium, raw athletic goodness to help me come Field Day. Along with Christmas and the NFL Draft, Field Day was my most favorite day of the year.

So Blake and I were tossing around a football, and Daniel wanted in. We obliged because, why not? After all, if a tentative, unspoken peace can't be brokered over football, haven't the terrorists already won? Before I knew it, we were blissfully tossing the ole pigskin around. Just three red-blooded boys engaged in a highly chill game of catch.

Except soon, Daniel threw a variable into the mix by catching the ball from Blake but not throwing it to me.

                        BLAKE and KNOX
        (Exchange looks as if to say, "What's this
        guy's deal?")

                           DANIEL
        (Throws the football in the air to himself,
        like a cat passive-aggressively playing
        with another cat's toy and begging for a
        confrontation.)

                           KNOX
                      (Taking the bait)

        Hey Daniel, super quick question: How
        about we keep this highly chill game
        of catch going and you resume tossing
        me the football?

                           DANIEL
                     (Thoughtful pause)

        Nah. I don't think so.

BLAKE and KNOX

(Exchange another look as if to say, "Can
you believe this guy's deal right now?")

KNOX

(Walks over to Daniel)

Dude, c'mon. Throw it to me or give it
back to me so we can throw the ball.

DANIEL

(Thoughtfully considers these options as if
he's a CPA considering property depreciation)

No, I don't think I want to do either
of those things.

KNOX

Okay then, here's the deal—

And right then, Daniel punched me in the nose, which is the second most annoying place to get punched.[5] The nose is particularly annoying because it bleeds and your eyes water. So not only is there bloody evidence of you getting a beatdown, but it also looks like you have been brought to tears. It's the equivalent to getting a wedgie on your face—the attack itself is less painful than the humiliation.

To sum up: blood gushed out of my nose, Daniel ran off with

---

5. The fourth most annoying place to get punched is the stomach because you can't breathe or talk. The third is the ear because it disorients you. The first (for dudes) is in the below-the-belt biscuits, for very obvious reasons.

our ball, our highly chill game of catch was over, and I realized I didn't take punches like Rocky took punches.

In retrospect I can say that this was the first significant conflict of my life, which I know makes me an incredibly privileged person. I accept that characterization with no protest.

Part of this delayed "trauma" is because I come from a privileged home situation and background. But also because, in terms of personality type, I was a pretty low-key kid. I eagerly avoided conflict and reprimand. Even now, I get stressed about something as dumb as walking into Target through the exit door because I assume a Red Shirt is going to swoop in and reprimand me for it.[6] My default is simply to avoid conflict.

The exception has always been sports. In the arena of athletic contests, I transformed into a Tasmanian devil of jerky-ness. You take someone who is hypercompetitive, petty, and sensitive, then add a healthy dose of the male ego and, boy oh boy, do you have a potent gumbo of emotional instability on your hands.

But outside of sports, I was very reserved, and I remain so to this day. And to be honest, I don't mind this aspect of myself. But not so much after experiencing my first face punch.

I was stunned with the knowledge that a punch-taking Rocky Balboa I was not. But even more affecting was my response—or lack thereof. Daniel just walking away with my football and face-punching virginity and me taking no recourse was just not the narrative I had anticipated for myself. I'd assumed I would be like, if not Rocky, Arnold Schwarzenegger from the Terminator movies. I would have expected to handle the situation with Daniel like this:

---

6. In reality, I know that, in my experience, most Red Shirts at Target wouldn't even intervene if I were performing an animal sacrifice in the greeting card aisle.

EXT. DARK ALLEY—NIGHT

There I am, shirtless, ripped, and wearing sunglasses despite it being night. Around me, trash cans billow with fire. Daniel refuses to throw me the football, so I activate my Terminator eye and confront him. He tries to sass me, then lands a punch, but it doesn't even hurt despite drawing a little blood.

I slowly wipe the blood from my nose with the back of my hand and say something awesome that sounds part hiss, part threat, and part Voltaire . . .

KNOX

No one makes me bleed my own blood.

. . . before counterpunching Daniel into infinity and retrieving the football as he flies into an endless vortex of regret for having ever stepped to me.

But I did none of these things. There was no infinity punching and there weren't even trash cans billowing with fire because that would have been so against the HOA of Blake's neighborhood.

As you can tell, getting punched in the face was a formative experience for me. As is getting hit with the revelation that expectation isn't reality. My expectation of how I would react to conflict had been influenced by pop culture; and, as I would find out, life didn't always go down like that.

Even at age ten, many aspects of my life—including my

faith—showed the influence of pop culture. My first visualized manifestation of God was George Burns. Somehow, around age six, I came into contact with his performance as God in *Oh, God!,* and I internalized it. Why, I have no idea. But it stuck. He's still my default avatar for God to this day.

I can only imagine that by this same logic, there are generations of kids who, when they think about God, might visualize Morgan Freeman from *Bruce Almighty* or the disembodied face from Monty Python. If this is true, I'm very jealous of those kids. Specifically the Morgan-Freeman-as-God kids. My vision of God is a guy who is like a million years old and looks like he smells like the Great Depression. Their vision is the guy who narrated *March of the Penguins* and who helps Bruce Wayne gear up for awesome Batman missions. Advantage: not me.

Of course, if we consider the inverse of this idea, that also suggests there may be a generation of kids who think of Al Pacino in *The Devil's Advocate* as Satan. For me, seeing Al Pacino depict Beelzebub didn't really stick, mostly because I was fourteen when *The Devil's Advocate* came out in theaters. And because it was rated R, I totally did not watch it (wink) when it came to TV a few years later. But primarily, I'd already imagined Satan's physical essence as vaguely red, pitchforky, and low-key snarly.[7]

This feels like a good spot to emphasize something important to know about me: I'm addicted to analogies. They're my go-to hack for making sense of the world. I just take the thing I don't understand and hold it up against things I do understand until I find some sort of clarity (thus God as George Burns).

---

7. These days, I assume Satan looks like (or is actually) Tilda Swinton. I say that with respect to all parties.

But when you always need other examples to explain the immediate thing you're trying to understand, this has the potential for intellectual disaster.

In the movie *Talladega Nights: The Legend of Ricky Bobby,* Will Ferrell's Ricky Bobby tries to prove that he is paralyzed by sticking a knife in his leg. He's trying (and failing) to show he can't feel the pain—and then the knife gets stuck. So Ricky Bobby uses another knife to try to unstick the first knife, but then that knife *also* gets stuck, compounding the problem. This is the same kind of problem I run into from time to time if the elements in my analogies don't completely land. If you don't fundamentally understand the first thing, your understanding of the second thing will always be compromised.

For example, in church I learned about a myriad of people in the Bible, but that didn't mean I understood them. I just had a name, an action, and every now and then their motivation. To me, they were all mostly flat characters. And though I was flatly earnest, this left me unable to grasp whatever spiritual application I was supposed to be taking from the story. That is, until I created real-world analogies using the lens I was most familiar with as a child: sports. It was then that these flat caricatures became round dynamos of complication and motivation.

- **God: ESPN.** I know, I know. This is probably sacrilegious. So I'll give you a moment to unclutch your pearls. In my defense, when I was a kid, ESPN seemed omnipresent, covering all aspects of sports, and their roster of talking heads projected a sense of omniscience. Truly, ESPN was the alpha and omega of the sports world, and Dan Patrick and Keith Olbermann were its prophets.
- **Jesus: Michael Jordan.** This is *definitely* sacrilegious, especially given our unlayering of MJ's, shall we say, complicated

history with vices, monogamy, and friendships. But consider the evidence:

- Like Jesus, Michael Jordan led a group of dedicated disciples: Scottie Pippen, B. J. Armstrong, John Paxson, Steve Kerr, and Luc Longley.
- Both were capable of miracles: Jesus walked on water, and MJ dunked from the free-throw line.
- Both confronted the authorities *a lot*: Jesus with the Sanhedrin and MJ with the refs.
- Both rose from the dead: Jesus after his crucifixion, and MJ resurrected his basketball career after spending a year swinging at—and missing—sliders.

- **Holy Spirit: Dick Vitale.** Simply put, there was no one else in my life with as much spirited enthusiasm for sports. He was an early draft of the modern hype man caricature. I couldn't always understand the words he was saying, which reminded me of what I'd learned about Pentecost. "Dipsy doo dunka-roo" seems perfectly at home in the larger linguistic madness that was Pentecost.

- **Cain and Abel: Tonya Harding and Nancy Kerrigan.** Like Abel, Nancy Kerrigan had a better public persona offering for the American people. Like Cain, Tonya Harding was so enraged at her rival's success that she participated in a conspiracy to assault.

- **Moses: Kirby Puckett.** Like Moses, Kirby Puckett was an unconventional hero. He was built like a pug but could run, and he had a penchant for clutchness in leading the Minnesota Twins to the promised land of World Series glory against my childhood team, the Atlanta Braves.

- **Judas: Hulk Hogan.** I'm still not ready to discuss the night

Hulk Hogan savagely betrayed Sting and Macho Man and joined New World Order, turning his back on all that was good about professional wrestling.

I'm aware this method was flawed in its oversimplification of many very complicated elements, but it did succeed in giving me a kind of shorthand in understanding the whole Christianity thing. I realize now that this impulse of using something secular to better understand the divine was the primordial soup from which my tendency to want to reconcile my experiences with my faith arose.[8]

As a kid, I was told about these supreme beings and legendary biblical characters who were responsible for articulating all good and all evil. That's kind of a big deal, so of course I'd want to characterize them. Maybe God is more appropriately described as a benevolent animating force intertwined with all our souls, or as a literal flame in a bush from the Moses burning bush story. But, guys, kids can't really unfurl the tableau of God manifestations so good, so George Burns it was.

That's what I remember from my elementary school years: having ideas impressed upon me, not knowing how to handle their bigness, and filling in the blanks the best way I knew how. I made sense of the world using elements of popular culture because I could access them easily, and this felt like an inroad through the seeming inaccessibility of knowing who I was and what I believed and whether or not the formation of these identities could sustain all the punches that would invariably come my way.

---

8. We're all very chill about me using an evolution reference to clarify my evangelical faith, right? Right.

Postscript to My First Punch in the Face

INT. OFFICE—LATE EVENING

It's twenty-one years after the events of Knox's first face punch. He is alone in his office, dutifully working on serious paperwork. Imagine lots of paper clips and manila folders. And hole punchers too. You can't even believe how many manila folders and hole punchers there are.

Anyway, his phone DINGS, indicating a text message. He rubs his weary eyes and retrieves the phone from the corner of his desk, grateful for a distraction from the contents of all those manila folders I just told you about.

The text is from his mom.

MOM

Guess whose mugshot I just found?[9]

KNOX
(Knox texts back.)

Who?

MOM

Mom texts back just a screenshot of none other than Former Face-Puncher, Daniel. At once, Knox is thrust into a cyclone of emotions. He

---

9. My mom scans the jail docket on the regular to find out who is getting arrested locally. It might be my favorite nonmaternal thing about her.

feels a twinge of empathy for the author of his first sucker punch, but also sadness at the passage of time and how it has the ability to neuter hope in all of us.

Another DING indicating another text message from his mom.

MOM

lol who saw that coming?

two

The Illusion of Pee-wee Herman

When I was eight, my uncle Tim told me the most revolutionary thing I'd heard up to that point. Granted, I was eight, so it's not like I'd heard of string theory or the theory that Katy Perry is really just grown-up JonBenét Ramsey. But still, what he told me was crazy even then. It was that Uncle Tim wasn't just Uncle Tim; he was also Pee-wee Herman. As in, Pee-wee from the Playhouse. Pee-wee of the Big Adventure.

This was mind-bending to say the least. Not just because Uncle Tim and Pee-wee Herman looked nothing alike, but because Pee-wee Herman was one of my first ride-or-die TV-show characters. I was in on the whole Pee-wee Herman vibe, worldview, and aesthetic. We're talking about a guy who had a live-in genie named Jambi who would grant him one wish per day. It would appear that Pee-wee Herman had life pretty well figured out. And then, all of a sudden, my uncle Tim was very casually revealing to me that I'm blood of Pee-wee?[1]

---

1. Technically I wouldn't have been direct royal blood to Pee-wee Herman since Uncle Tim married my mom's sister, but it was close enough for me.

The important thing to understand here is that at the time of this revelation, my uncle Tim was six foot four, 220 pounds, and a member of the US military. And he *looked* like he was a member of the military—not like one of those guys about whom you might wonder, *Is he in the military or does he work at Build-A-Bear? I can't quite decide.*

No, Uncle Tim looked like he could have been in the cast photo of *G. I. Joe.* Imagine a group of soldiers in army barracks getting rowdy around an arm-wrestling match. Any of the guys in your head right now probably looks like my uncle Tim.

Pee-wee Herman, in contrast to Uncle Tim, looked to be about five foot five and maybe 125 pounds soaking wet—like the kind of guy who counts soup as a meal and is always wistfully looking at the thermostat, wishing he could turn it up at least five degrees higher.[2]

Eventually though, I learned the truth about this explosive claim. Uncle Tim wasn't Pee-wee Herman. He wasn't Tom or Jerry or Garfield or Slimer or any other of my favorite Saturday-morning cartoon characters. He was just Uncle Tim.

This experience was huge for two main reasons. First, this was my first experience of someone in authority lying to me. Which doesn't sound that important especially given what was lied about, but this moment's importance is more about what existed beyond the lie.

As kids, we slowly broaden our circles of understanding until we have a pretty good handle on things. But that's a lot more difficult than it seems because we're all born in the middle of everything. An entire world is happening around us, and as young humans

---

2. I could easily verify some of this information, but there was no Wikipedia when I was a kid, so I feel like collectively my generation's instincts are pretty great on people's sizing.

we've just got to figure out how to jump onto an intellectual merry-go-round that's going two hundred miles per hour. That's why childhood isn't really the time for challenging convention, but rather acclimating to it.

As kids, we're all conscripted into the institutions of belief and identity around us before we're equipped to grasp what we're buying into. For me, the institutions I built my life around were the local Baptist church, sports, and the South. And exactly none of those institutions were choices I had agency in opting into, because I didn't have any agency about anything yet. It's not like I was on the fence about whether to become a Buddhist or Baptist. I was a kid. I wanted to have my birthday party at McDonald's four years in a row. What did I know about anything?

In this respect, think about the institution of Santa Claus. The whole Santa mirage is an elaborate case study of cultural entrapment from the word *go*. We're born, we start to learn what the world is about, and then suddenly we're told by the people we love and trust (and reinforced by media messaging) that there's this magical, chubby immortal who monitors our behavior and rewards us with gifts if we act right. And that's pretty much the biggest headline-grabbing supernatural fact to exist in our lives up to that point. Finding out about the existence and purpose of Santa Claus takes every single slice of every single cake that has ever existed.

I know some of you just read this and are pushing your Christian nerd glasses up the bridge of your nose, saying, "But Knox, the biggest headline grab for kids should be about God and how he's omnipotent and infinite and omnipresent."

Yeah, yeah, settle down. I know that you *think* he should be, but that's just not the case. Sure, God eventually becomes the bigger headline, but expecting young children to understand the implications and existential nuances of God (especially in comparison to the simplicity of Santa Claus) is like trying to explain the stock market to your golden retriever.[3]

For kids, accessing an idea like Santa is so much easier because it is directly related to them. They see the Santa charade played out once a year in a gloriously decadent morning of toy bliss. That first Christmas morning as children when we're intellectually with it and putting things together? That's when everything locks into place and we decide that Santa Claus, as dubious as his realness might be, was definitely in the building, because we get all that circumstantial evidence. I mean, the cookies had bites taken out of them. The milk clearly quenched a holiday thirst. That's an attention to detail that our little minds could not overlook.

And why would we even think to overlook this evidence? Probably because for children to consider Santa's unrealness is so prohibitively terrifying and nihilistic that we reflexively reject it. To go down that road as a kid requires us to consider that we've been victimized by this elaborate, culturally cohesive long con. A long con, mind you, that we did not opt into. Which is why I think we naturally repel this implication, because it suggests:

- We cannot trust those we love and trust the most.
- We were entrapped into believing something that was utter fiction with the understanding that the uncovering of the deception would always be an uneven, unsteadying process because

---

3. The machinations of the stock market and how they relate to your 401(k) and savings account may correlate directly to the quality of dog toys, food, and treats he gets—but he's a *dog*, you guys. He wants tennis balls, two squares a day, and maybe a strange leg to hump every now and again.

- the potency of the charade had worn off to the point that our doubts and skepticism counterbalanced our belief over the course of a prolonged intellectual struggle;
- one or more of our peers humiliated us with the truth, usually in a social setting; or
- we jarringly discovered evidence of the complicity of our parents in service to the lie.

Now, I realize that as a culture we're all too invested in the Santa Industrial Complex to ever be a post-Santa society.[4] It's just not happening, and I'm not arguing for it to happen. My wife, Ashley, and I have continued the lie with our kids even though I'm an authentically terrible liar (which is why I try not to ever play poker or talk to pregnant women).

But I'm illustrating the vividness of pure, uncut belief. As kids, we freebase belief because we have no experience or reason to question it. Our suspension of disbelief isn't even a suspension; the mechanism itself doesn't even exist yet. It's just 100 percent trust because, why wouldn't it be? Most of us were fortunate enough to have not had that trust violated during childhood.

But sometimes, that trust is loudly violated, and we quickly get acquainted with the idea that not all ideas or people are trustworthy. But the more fortunate of us can slowly watch that idea unravel.

For example, with Santa Claus, there's a real effort to conceal the truth; but when it comes to the Tooth Fairy or the Easter Bunny, parents all seem to have a laissez-faire approach to those charades.

---

4. I believed in Santa for an insanely long time. Like, longer than you are thinking. As in, take the age you are assuming for me and add two to three years, and you *probably* have how old I was.

INT. LIVING ROOM—MORNING

A bedroom door swings open; Knox's six-year-old explodes through the door after a complete night of sleep.

SIX-YEAR-OLD

(Apoplectic and yelling)

DADDY! WHERE IS MY MONEY?

KNOX

(Knowing he forgot to leave out money)

There wasn't money?

SIX-YEAR-OLD

This is three days now the Tooth Fairy has forgotten me. *(Beat)* I'm not someone she wants to be forgetting.

KNOX

Wasn't it a holiday last night? Tooth fairies don't work holidays.

SIX-YEAR-OLD

That was two days ago.

KNOX

(Knowing the tooth was clearly displayed)

Did you have the tooth clearly displayed?

SIX-YEAR-OLD

OF COURSE I HAD IT DISPLAYED. It sat atop the bedazzled Play-Doh tower I built PRECISELY for her to see.

KNOX

Maybe we could write a letter to the Tooth Fairy's supervisor?

SIX-YEAR-OLD

I thought you said tooth fairies work alone?

KNOX
(Scrambling)

Uh, they do work alone, but also together. Like in a union. Or a freelance collective.

SIX-YEAR-OLD
(Turns to leave room)

You should probably get your story straight, Daddy.

Like a piñata, the ideas of Santa, the Tooth Fairy, and the Easter Bunny all exist to be eventually broken. And in a sense, whatever initial beliefs we are conscripted into function like that too. And while I don't think the foundation of these beliefs are necessarily meant to be broken beyond repair like our belief, say, in the Easter

Bunny, I do think we're meant to break with the simplistic terms in which we understand these massively complicated ideas.

Throughout a large part of my childhood, the movie *Pee-wee's Big Adventure* was constantly in the rewatch rotation for me and my sister, Laura. In the beginning of this bizarre movie, Pee-wee has this amazing bike that is stolen from him, and he spends the rest of the movie trying to get it back. He fights through crazy hijinks and uncomfortable situations, all in pursuit of the bike. Eventually, he regains it with a new appreciation for it and for the things he experienced along the way.

In a lot of ways, the process of understanding my belief and faith and God has felt like that for me. It was something I held in my heart from a very young age; and while I never lost it or had it taken from me, I couldn't help but notice how both it and I were changing. And it has been during this process of change that I realized how you can be grateful for something while also being occasionally discontent with it.

And if you're wondering how I figured out that Uncle Tim wasn't Pee-wee Herman, I actually never did. My mom revealed the truth to me in 1991 after the guy who portrayed Pee-wee (Paul Reubens) was arrested for exposing himself inside a New York adult theatre. Evidently, it's all fun and games until the guy your uncle claims to be gets arrested for pleasuring himself in public.

three

High Stakes

You're probably picking up on the fact that I consider myself a Christian. I realize the whole Christian thing might make some flinch because it comes complete with a complicated set of expectations, politics, behaviors, and proximity to Kirk Cameron.

In this way, being labeled a Christian can be a lot like being labeled patriotic or a conspiracy theorist. None of these designations are inherently bad, but they can easily tend toward the negative after some of the more cliché interactions with people under their banner.

As a culture, I think we've all dealt with

- the very awkward and presumptive person confronting you (read: wanting to Jesus-ambush you) about your eternal destiny;
- the person who thinks the planes on 9/11 were just holograms and that the whole thing was an inside job by Beyoncé, Jay-Z, and the Knights Templar; and
- the person who has a tattoo of a bald eagle, in flight, holding the Constitution in one talon and Abraham Lincoln in the other, who is looking menacingly upon any NFL player who dares not stand for the national anthem.

There's an adverse reaction to spending even a few moments with these kinds of people, and that is totally fair. But, in general, in a large enough subset of experiences, you will encounter one bad egg from within any label. This includes Buddhist monks, grandmas, and even Chick-fil-A employees.[1]

Even though I'm a card-carrying evangelical Christian,[2] trust me when I say that this book isn't a low-key effort to be like *To Catch a Predator*, wherein I burst into the consciousness of your soul and, over the course of these pages, make you accept your salvation from Jesus Christ.[3] At points in my youth, I was very much that person—and with the benefit of hindsight, I've developed some, uh, complicated feelings about that behavior and history. Instead, my goal here is to perform something of a spiritual audit of my own faith experience. (Or at least that's what my editor tells me. I'm really just here to make a ton of references to *Saved by the Bell* and hope for the best.)

I realize that makes us strange bookfellows. I mean, why should you care about me putting my faith under a microscope? That feels kind of intimate, no? Well, I guess what I'm hoping for is that you get from this what I get from watching *The Profit*.

For context, *The Profit* is a reality show starring Actual Rich Guy Marcus Lemonis. In each episode, he decides whether to invest in businesses that are in operational or financial trouble. To make his decision, he considers three principles: people, product, and process. In other words, are the people at the company hardworking, is

---

1. I know. I've never actually had a bad experience with a Chick-fil-A employee; but on an infinite scale, science suggests that at least one negative interaction has to occur.

2. Just kidding—we don't carry cards. Too mark-of-the-Beasty.

3. What would this show be called? *To Convert a Heathen*? *To Catch a Convert*? Also I can't believe this isn't already a show on a Christian TV network.

the product viable and profitable, and are there processes in place for success? Once he identifies which of these things are broken, he takes steps to right the company, and there is much entrepreneurial rejoicing.

I like *The Profit* because it's a good show, but also because I find Marcus's thoughtful approach to business applicable to many areas of my life, especially my faith. When our faith isn't as strong as it could be, where have we gone wrong? Is it the people, the product, or the process? How do we right what's broken if we don't first examine it?

And I realize I'm very casually tossing around the word *faith* as though we all distinctly understand what it means. To clarify, my use of *faith* is a generalized shorthand for everything encompassing my religious beliefs. In other words, faith is a lot like Mary Poppins's purse: very simple idea, deeply complicated contents.

As you will see in this book, at times my good-faith effort at good faith goes wildly off the rails. And when I try to figure out exactly how that happened, it's contextually important to go back to my earliest memories of attending church on Sunday mornings.

In terms of Sunday church attendance, generally speaking, there are two sections of church to participate in: Sunday school or the worship service. In scholastic terms, the worship service is like the college intro to psychology class with hundreds of students, where no attendance is taken.

Sunday school, on the other hand, is like the class very much up the rear[4] of your major that you take in the first semester of your senior year. Like Adolescent British Literature Absurdism Theory. Attendance *is* taken and you *are* expected to participate.

Traditionally, our church experience consisted of starting with

---

4. Because I wasn't allowed to say the word that rhymes with *butt*.

Sunday school, then going to the worship service before retreating to various chain restaurant outposts to finish off the first half of our Sunday. But this has diversified wildly over the last decade or so. Now a lot of churches offer multiple services because they are sensitive to families like mine that are a bit of a disaster when it comes to arriving at the house of God on time.

Personally, I always like going to the worship service last because this is like the great Christian *kaboom* kickstarting the week. It's like *Soul Train* for your soul, minus any and all provocative dancing. You hear a helpful, instructive message to help send you off into the week with a great mind-set.

What's more, the worship service is also like a weekly convention featuring the entire pastoral gang. Did you ever watch the *Captain Planet* cartoons? Whenever the Planeteers got together and used their rings to summon Captain Planet ("By your powers combined!"), big things happened. And that's basically what this service is—all the pastors using their pastoral superpowers together to make big things happen.

> The Pastor Who Deals with the Sermons
> The Pastor Who Deals with the Music
> The Pastor Who Deals with Details
> The Pastor Who Deals with Old People
> The Pastor Who Deals with Young People
> The Pastor Who Deals with Children
> The Pastor Who Deals with Single People
> The Pastor Who Deals with Technology

Basically any kind of pastor you can think of, they are in this service.

Now, all this existed in my life before the modern proliferation of children's church programs. Today, you walk into a church and there's an entire Narnia unto itself of classes, activities, and curriculum catering to kids. Each class has a sort of religious au pair, and every fifteen minutes they get warm towels and a food cart full of those little shot glasses with different desserts crammed into them. It's truly an incredible time to be a child in modern American churches.

My experience was a little bit different, though. When I was a kid, Sunday school—or "Little Church," as my family called it—was kind of like that room from the original *Saw* movie, but with less blood and maybe one more window. From time to time, some stale Goldfish crackers were thrown into the room, leading to near riots. The extent of our entertainment options where two wooden puzzles, both missing one to three pieces each.

Today, though, each kid gets their own VR headset transporting them to ancient Jerusalem where they can watch Jesus perform miracles from the perspective of one of the lesser disciples like Bartholomew.[5] But not so much back in my day. To be fair, I wouldn't have wasted budget money on me and my peer group either. After all, I was a child who counted Bozo the Clown as one of my biggest influences, and my hashtag-goals and main aspiration in life was to compete in the Grand Prize Game.[6] I was so dumb, I didn't even want to win the Grand Prize Game; I just wanted to compete in it. ("Just happy to be here, Bozo!") So why dedicate a

---

5. When you think of Bartholomew's place within the disciple crew, think the Michelle of this divine Destiny's Child situation.

6. Bozo's Grand Prize Game was the challenge of tossing a Ping-Pong ball in a series of six buckets. If you hit all six, you'd win cash, a bike, and a trip somewhere.

significant line item in the budget to this clearly idiotic subset of the church population?

This is probably a good time to reveal that I hated church as a kid. Not because I was a Wiccan or anything, and not because I expected a luxurious, first-class Sunday school experience. Primarily, it was due to the dichotomy of what church was. All the observable behavior about church communicated to me that it was awesome! And the best! But it usually only succeeded in being mostly boring, except when Old Testament Bible stories were told, which were thrilling, but in a macabre, horrifying kind of way that secretly traumatized me.

These stories stood in stark contrast to my preferred story delivery context, *He-Man and the Masters of the Universe*. For the unfamiliar, *He-Man and the Masters of the Universe* starred a guy named Prince Adam who, when he held the Sword of Power aloft and uttered the words, "By the power of Grayskull!" became He-Man and would receive "fabulous secret powers."

The success of this cartoon, to me, was that it succeeded in being accessibly mysterious. Questions like, "Who is Grayskull?" and "Why didn't Prince Adam always hold that sword aloft and just stay He-Man in perpetuity?" nagged at me, but they didn't unravel the context because I was already having a good time. Broadly, we tend not to pick at things when we're having a good time. This is why early seasons of *LOST* were great but later ones became tedious. This is also why we never question the existence of God after winning the lottery or getting picked to play in Bozo the Clown's Grand Prize Game.

Even when faced with *He-Man*'s distinctly disconnected vocabulary like "fabulous secret powers," I didn't mind. Objectively, the word *fabulous* being used in any kind of proximity to superheroes is bizarre. Can you imagine Spiderman shooting one of his *fabulous* webs, Batman using a Fab-arang or *The Fabulously Incredible Hulk*? But it didn't matter because the show and the process of experiencing it had curried my favor.

To this point, other elements of the show definitely stick out to me now, like the doubly masculine moniker of "He-Man." Like, we get it; you're an alpha male—but part of these fabulous and secret powers you are getting makes you become like, I dunno, a double dude?[7]

But let's talk more about the main villain, Skeletor. The great thing about this guy was that he didn't leave me wondering about his antihero potential. My six-year-old brain never had to wrestle with the idea, *Is Skeletor unredeemable OR is Skeletor a good skeleton who repeatedly does bad things?* while indulging in a post-episode juice box. Skeletor was just a straight-up bad guy. Evil voice, evil skull face, and evil deeds.

Sure, there were all kinds of stories and motivations festooning the fringes of this animated delight, but when it got down to the brass tacks of He-Man versus Skeletor, everything was all pretty straightforward. He-Man is a handsome (though with a tragically bad haircut) hero-made-manifest super double dude, and my guy Skeletor is just a hooded skeleton. He's literally stripped of his humanity. He's just bones and bad intentions. He wants to rule Eternia, get some of those "fabulous secret powers," and wreck stuff, full stop.

The people, the product, and the process of *He-Man* all lined

---

7. Those little flourishes aren't the only dissonant elements of the story. I mean, the main villain himself is a skeleton shrouded within a closeting suit of masculinity. And let's just say that if I had a nickel for every phallic symbol included in the story, I'd be an individual with a great many nickels.

up for me. But when it came to the Bible stories I learned about in Sunday school? I just wasn't about that Old Testament life yet.

For example, I will never forget going to church and hearing the story about Abraham getting ready to sacrifice his son, Isaac, to God. In my heart there was terror, and in my brain there was a record-scratch noise. I played back all the info I'd gathered. "So wait, Abraham is the dad, which makes Isaac the son. And God is God. But God also wants Abraham to kill Isaac? Sorry, what now?"

This was like *The Sixth Sense* but for Sunday school because I was very much not ready for such a plot twist. I was relieved to find out that God was just testing Abraham, but I wasn't *that* relieved. The fact that I had been taken to the point of being relieved that God didn't make a father murder his son limited the fullness of the relief I could experience.

But I just told myself that they all probably had a huge LOL after the fact, did a freeze-frame group high five, and all lived (mostly) happily ever after—except, perhaps, for the PTSD Isaac had and the permanent dread associated with his having lost faith in his father as a caregiver. But other than that, I was sure everything was totally fine.

But not so much for me. Nothing was fine. I couldn't put this story away. It raised more questions in my young mind than it answered. I suddenly looked at my own father with very suspicious eyes. I considered the sacrificial leanings of various family members. My dad didn't seem like he had it in him. My mom, though, might have been a different story—but only in regard to my sister, who liked to routinely familiarize herself with the boundaries of parental rules and frequently stress-test the structural integrity of those boundaries. This led to a great many disagreements, and it left me wondering what my mom would do in a situation similar to Abraham's.

INT. BEDROOM—EVENING

Mom is prayerfully knelt; God is in heaven, working on world peace, etc.

MOM

Say, God, quick question. Any chance you need me to sacrifice my daughter?

GOD

(Looks up, somewhat startled)

You're asking if you need to sacrifice your daughter, like, to prove your commitment to me?

MOM

Yeah, yeah, sure. Something like that.

GOD

You know? I think I'm good actually. No sacrifices needed here.

MOM

(Trying to hide her disappointment, but she can't)

Wow. Really? You're sure?

GOD

Am . . . Am I sure that I don't want you to sacrifice your daughter?

MOM

Yeah.

GOD

Pretty sure about that. Besides, that was Old Testament me. Those people weren't very artsy so they needed vivid and direct demonstrations of me. I think your generation of people get what I'm going for, for the most part.

MOM

Counterpoint: Maybe we don't. Maybe we could use some of the old-time religion, know what I'm saying?

GOD

I gotta say, it really just feels like you want to sacrifice your daughter.

MOM
(Theatrical disbelief)

What? Me? What? That's just a really, really crazy thing to say.

(A pause. God is clearly ready to leave, but Mom is still trying to keep the conversation thread open.)

MOM

Buuuuuuuuut (*letting it hang there for a minute*) you have to admit, the more you think about it, the more interesting the idea becomes, right?

GOD

I think we're done here.

The thought refused to go away. I couldn't stop wondering about whether or not my sister or I might end up as collateral damage in a faith test. And even more, I worried that if this kind of test did happen, what if God got distracted by a famine, a hurricane, or a Super Bowl, and forgot to tell my mom or dad that he was just kidding?

On a fundamental level, I loved God. But on that same level, I also wasn't 100 percent sure I could trust him.[8]

And why should I, when every story I was hearing made him out to be an omnipotent super villain with a penchant for wrath, flood, and fire? Turning Lot's wife into a pillar of salt when she looked back on an exploding city—that is some Jafar-at-the-end-of-*Aladdin* stuff. Between learning these stories in Sunday school and seeing *Raiders of the Lost Ark,* I began to question, what was God's deal with not looking at things? Why make all these incredible destruction sequences and magical covenants that can melt Nazi faces, and a tree with knowledge of good and evil, if you don't want humans to be insanely interested in these things? You *know* that only makes us want it that much more.

---

8. This is very similar to how I feel now about Ryan Reynolds. Love his humor and personality, but can we trust his taste in movies outside *Deadpool?* IMDB suggests no.

I'd be lying if I said I wasn't horrifically enthralled in the miasma of Old Testament cautionary tales, but it also left me feeling unmoored. I couldn't look away, but I also couldn't shake the feeling that this couldn't *really* be God, right?

Somehow I was expected to not only trust this God, but also give my heart to him—a point my pastor drove home in every single worship service. And credit where credit is due, my pastor was a master of the evangelical call to action (a.k.a. the altar call).

The altar call itself is typically an invitation directly following the message where a hymn like "I Have Decided to Follow Jesus" softly plays underneath a pastor's formal invitation to come down to the altar to ask Jesus to live inside your heart.

My pastor's strategy was a master class in setting up a call to action. He motivated it by identifying the high stakes that were involved. The call to action was accepting salvation (or leading others to salvation), and the motivation was the difference between eternal, sulfuric, demon-proctored torment amid hellfire—and a paradise full of golden streets, no pain, no suffering, and fellowship with God, Jesus, and the rest of the Awesome Bible Characters gang.

If I'm being completely transparent, as a kid, one of my big concerns about heaven was that it was always pitched to me to be like one giant worship service, which sounded super counterintuitive. "An eternal church worship service? *That's* heaven? Really?" To be honest, that sounded less like heaven and more like the other place. The truest iteration of heaven to me at that point would have been a giant swimming pool full of McDonald's chicken nuggets, lots of sports, family, friends, and playing Bozo the Clown's Grand Prize Game. Probably a lazy river thrown in too. And maybe a domesticated velociraptor that could also play *Contra* with me when I needed a wingman. We're getting offtrack, but you get the point:

pretty much at the bottom of my wish list for heaven was an eternal worship service. But any hesitations about heaven were erased by my very unhesitant fear of hell. Hymns and exegetical studies on the New Testament weren't ideal, but they were certainly better than eternal demonic torture.

And my pastor's evangelical finishing move tapped directly into that simplicity of thought: "If you died tonight, where would you go?"

Sometimes this question would be heightened by adding more detail. "If you left here tonight and got into a fatal car wreck/had a piano fall on your dang head/got stepped on by an elephant and lost your life, where would you go?" But it always boiled things down to the zero-sum game at the heart of my faith.

My pastor's mastery of service punctuation is the reason I accepted Jesus into my heart more than five thousand times.[9] When the stakes are that stark, you kind of want to be sure that you won't be downgraded to the lake of fire due to a technicality.

The way I related to salvation—as a get-out-of-hell-free card rather than as a gift of abundant life—tells you everything needed to know about adolescent me, especially against the backdrop of my horrified fascination with the violence of the Old Testament. The stakes for me were simple, primal, and horrific, and the echoes of that understanding will always have a compartment in my consciousness, no matter how deeply I bury it.

Along these lines, I don't think we make enough of a fuss over the distillation of the gospel into "For your eternity, will you be choosing sanctified or chicken fried? Are you getting right or getting

---

9. This feels like hyperbole, no? Well, buckle your believability belts because it's actually not. I've been saved more than all the blonde white women in all the action movies ever combined.

left?" There's nothing holy or redeeming in a choice out of fear of the alternative. Even if that did seem to jibe with the God I was learning about in Sunday school—a God who seemed to use fear as his go-to tactic—there was discord in my soul about wondering whether this was what my interpretation of God should really be. It's the same kind of dissonance we all feel when God is misrepresented by those advocating on behalf of corrosive and hateful things.

Marcus Lemonis would have seen it right away: my faith was true, and the people helping me build it were good, but my processing of it all? It wasn't quite there yet.

four

Knox McCoy, Canine Evangelist

If you watch enough movies and TV, you may have picked up on a shadow dynamic regarding animal protagonists. I call it the "Pyramid of Animal Deaths," and the basic gist is that certain fictional animals, just because of their species, subconsciously invest you in their survival. In other words, you either root for or against the animal based on cultural conditioning.

For example, think of Sir Hiss in Disney's animated *Robin Hood*. He's a tool of tyranny, a snitch, and in cahoots with the central antagonist of the movie, Prince John. That's enough to say that he just flat-out sucks. But also, he's a snake. So when he gets his comeuppance, there's no subconscious cultural conditioning to struggle with because he's a snake, and unless you are a frequent vaper with a chinstrap beard, we all agree that snakes are the worst. Partly because they are basically like, "What if worms were much bigger, more ambitious, and could kill you?" Also because of garden of Eden reasons.[1]

---

1. I have a spicy-hot religious take that it isn't even really the serpent's fault. It takes two to commit original sin, not just one crafty snake. And don't give me the "They didn't realize!" Are you kidding me? You're saying they weren't completely fascinated with the only thing in the world they couldn't partake in? Yeeaaaah, okay. The serpent is just a patsy and got an unnecessarily bad rap. That being said, snakes are the *worst*.

Conversely, something like a koala bear gets the benefit of the doubt because we've accepted them as just cuddly bears, and there's no preexisting subtext making them culpable for the fall of mankind. That makes them pretty sympathetic as story characters.

Let me take you through the levels of the pyramid so you can get a sense of what animals most people are pretty cool with getting iced versus which animal deaths could cause a riot.

JERKFACE DELUXE ANIMALS
(Bottom of the Pyramid)

This tier is reserved for animals people actively dislike and have no problem watching get got.

- **Rats.** Never forget the Black Death. I enjoyed *Ratatouille* as much as the next person, but be real, you guys; you'd rather eat a Band-Aid sandwich than something a rat lovingly concocted.
- **Snakes.** I literally just talked about this.
- **Spiders.** Entirely too many legs and eyes. Also, the urban legend about them laying eggs in your face didn't do their branding any favors.
- **Hyenas.** Because they tried to kill Simba and almost ruined Pride Rock.[2]
- **Octopi.** Too many tentacles. Why does any animal need that many tentacles? Aren't two tentacles sufficient? There's an obviously nefarious agency afoot (atentacle?) with these animals.
- **Crocodiles.** Prehistoric swamp-monster killing machines?

---

2. Another spicy take: the hyenas weren't that bad. Remember, all they wanted was to eat. Mufasa wouldn't let them eat and rudely didn't invite them to the super-cool Simba coronation dance party.

Extreme Randy Jackson from *American Idol* voice: "That's a no from me, dawg."

- **Sharks.** Even though they have their own week on the Discovery Channel, they still ruin beach trips and they're actively trying to ruin tornadoes. What is their problem?

LUKEWARM AFFECTION ANIMALS
(Middle of the Pyramid)

- **Camels.** They transport (cool) but also spit (*not* cool).
- **Kangaroos.** Kanga and Roo from *Winnie the Pooh* seem sweet, but in recent years, the internet has shown us entirely too many kangaroos that are ready to throw down.[3]
- **Monkeys.** They have the propensity to be cute but they also tend to ruin the sentiment of their cuteness with feces throwing. And, for a time, they were always the culprit when fictional pandemics got rolling. They better be thankful for the swine and bird flus; otherwise, monkeys would be full-blown problematic.
- **Birds.** There's a lot of back-and-forth with this animal. Alfred Hitchcock made them evil, but then they helped Noah know when the flood was over. You've got Big Bird[4] but also *Angry Birds*. Because of the many oppositional characterizations, it's enough to make them just lukewarm.

---

3. Are kangaroos Australia's version of the golden retriever? As in, the Air Bud series is to America as Kangaroo Jack is to Australia?

4. Isn't it crazy that Big Bird makes everyone on *Sesame Street* refer to him as Big Bird despite being the only bird around? What an aggressive stance, right? Seems indicative of extreme insecurity or someone very power hungry. Either way, I'll never look at him the same way.

MAXIMUM ELITE CUTENESS
(Top of the Pyramid)

- **Cats.** Because some people, who make bad decisions and struggle with self-loathing and masochistic tendencies, love them.
- **Rabbits.**[5] I would argue that the rabbit who was unceremoniously boiled in *Fatal Attraction* accomplished more for rabbits through that martyrdom than the Easter Bunny ever did.
- **Dogs.** The Babe Ruth of sympathetic animals.

We assign a lot of innocence to that Maximum Elite Cuteness tier of animals. Domesticated pets like cats and dogs and rabbits offer something approximating unconditional love[6] and serve as a salve when we're at our most vulnerable; they offer up snuggles and emotional comfort, especially in times when we're so sad that we eat two entire bags of Doritos while watching a *Property Brothers* marathon. We're uniquely invested in the survival of these animals because, in some ways, they also contribute to our emotional survival.

This idea wasn't limited to animals and pet ownership. At church, too, I was being primed to invest in the innocent, specifically when it came to helping other people find salvation. The emphasis wasn't so much on helping murderers, adulterers, and persecutors find Jesus; it was on introducing "innocent" people—people who didn't jaywalk, tipped handsomely, and said "excuse me" when they burped—to our whole Jesus situation.

---

5. We actually have a rabbit: Justin Thumperlake. He has zero personality, is very fat, and chews on the walls. Do not get a rabbit.

6. Really, it's probably more like hierarchal deference, but it *feels* like unconditional love, no?

As an elementary school kid, this was crazy stressful because I deeply felt the burden of needing to share the gospel with anyone ignorant of Jesus. I couldn't understand how this wasn't the only conversation all of us were having with anyone. It almost felt like a prerequisite to any interaction or conversation. And the immediacy of this impulse led directly to my backyard.

You should know: I'm a huge dog person. I have a huge soft spot in my heart for them. I won't watch a movie if I know a dog is going to die, because I can't put myself through that emotional torture again like I did in 1989 after seeing *All Dogs Go to Heaven.*

The timing could not have been more perfect. I loved animals, and every Sunday I was learning more and more about the reward of heaven and how important it was that I help people get there. *All Dogs Go to Heaven* became the perfect confluence of these two things. But just below the surface, there were some irreconcilable differences I had a hard time wrapping my head around.

If we agree with the precedent set by the movie, then the need for canine sanctification is moot because of the title alone. But this premise stood in stark contrast to what I was learning in church. There hadn't been anything in the New Testament about anyone getting a free pass, much less dogs. As far as I knew, Jesus was still the way, the truth, and the life—and that applied to dogs too. Which presented a litany of issues I had trouble understanding.

1. Can dogs read or understand the essence of the Bible?
2. Do dogs understand metaphors and, by extension, parables?
3. In terms of identifiable theology, do dogs have their own set of iconic figures setting their own kind of canine Christianity into motion *or* are they beholden to our construct of Christianity?

Even if I had bought into the cinematic precedent of free heavenly admission for dogs, there were still a ton of red flags suggesting that all was not as it seemed.

First, Burt Reynolds was the voice of Charlie B. Barkin,[7] the main dog protagonist. Now, I was just a child and not fully aware of Burt Reynolds's body of work, but I think some things transcend experiential awareness. Just like we are all born with some kind of sense of our Creator, I think we're also born assuming that Burt Reynolds has engaged in his fair share of morality-adjacent pursuits. We don't need to see the ugly details of how the sausage is womanized to intuitively know that, right?

Second, the story of *All Dogs Go to Heaven* didn't feel like it was being told through an evangelical-approved lens. The story takes place in a 1930s New Orleans casino, and though this is never explicitly stated, there's definitely an underworld/organized crime atmosphere going on.[8]

Lastly, the heaven illustrated in the movie didn't seem much like the one being advertised during Big Church services. I mean, there was a whippet dog playing the role of Saint Peter, which is *super* dubious because I think if dogs uniformly had to elect a particular breed as the representative sample of goodness greeting them as they shuffled off their mortal coils (leashes?) and entered into eternity, it would probably go:

1. **Golden retriever.** Might be more angelic than Saint Peter IMO.

---

7. Guys, can we just take a second and just luxuriate in the richness of that name?

8. The setting is deeply implied, and I actually appreciate that they left it to the subtext and didn't lean into it fully. It had the effect of leaving open the possibility of an *All Dogs Go to Heaven* expanded universe that I'm still waiting for.

2. **Labrador retrievers.** The all-American, apple pie–sniffing dog next door.
3. **Siberian huskies.** Those eyes tho.
4. **Beagle.** Scrappy, overachieving everydogs.
5. **German shepherd.** Would be higher but lost a ton of points thanks to an unfortunate connection to the Big Bads of World War II.
6. **Whippets.** They look like they are either embarking upon or just recovering from an intense drug habit.

Last Place: Corgis. These dogs are probably the gatekeepers to hell.[9] While cute, this dog is more useless than a urinal cake-flavored popsicle. My parents have had two of these dogs and all they were good at was being emotional terrorists. Zero stars, would not recommend.

Suffice it to say, I left that movie doubly traumatized. One, because Charlie was straight-up murdered. Two, because I realized that canine moral hall passes did not exist.

What an emotional crisis to try to solve on top of a heaping plate of preexisting spiritual crisis, right? You know that moment in life when you realize you're just a tiny lever in a compounding institutional mechanism? And that no matter how much you rage against the machine, nothing will change? That was me at seven in the realization that almost every dog I saw was going straight to hell. Unless I intervened.

So I accepted the call to become a sort of Billy Graham–like crusader/liaison to the dog world, dedicated to leading as many of

---

9. I know Greek myth says it's Cerberus, a giant, three-headed dog, and it makes no mention of dog breed, but I can guarantee you that Cerberus must have had three large and stupid corgi heads.

them to salvation as I could. I started with my own dog, Elway,[10] a mutt straight out of central casting.[11] She had the head of a shaggy lab on the body of a shrunken golden retriever. She was a stray who had wandered into our backyard and into the open arms of my mother, the patron saint of stray dogs, from whom I inherited my bleeding heart for canines.

Elway wasn't particularly loving or smart or protective of anyone besides my mom. Essentially, she skirted by solely because she was a dog and we were a family of dog lovers. If I had to draw a line between her and a modern celebrity, I would choose Dax Shepard— not especially amazing, but successful at being loyal to someone more powerful than himself.

So I began my evangelical experimentation with converting Elway to Christianity. At first, I would approach her and read from my Bible, hoping that the New Testament scriptures would majestically captivate her and allow me to lead her in the prayer of salvation. Very quickly, though, I could tell that she found the Bible to be noninteresting.

So I improvised and strategically deployed a dog treat to help garner her attention. But soon I realized her focus was on the temporal pleasures of the treat and not the eternal status of her heathen soul.

I tried giving her the treat and, while she chewed, I would pray with her and cover her eyes to feign a reciprocal prayerfulness. But, if you have any experience with dogs, you know that the last thing a dog wants when it is chewing is for an insane child to cover its

---

10. To this day, I still don't know why we landed on Elway. We weren't Broncos fans, and everyone knows that John Elway looks like a horse, not a dog.

11. A generational legacy of mutts, Elway's lineage could probably be traced back to some dumpy, short-legged-looking mutt running alongside woolly mammoths.

eyes and breathlessly recite the prayer of salvation. I didn't know this, though, and had my hands and face bitten more than a couple of times. But that was just my cross to bear as a canine missionary.

Finally, I landed on the winning combination. A no-strings-attached treat, followed by belly rubs while I whisper-yelled scriptures at her. Then I would try again to get close to her face and cover her eyes with my hand, praying on her behalf to accept Jesus as her personal Lord and Savior so she might spend eternity with God, me, and any other dogs I managed to convert.[12]

With the model proven and with experience as my guide, I set out to convert every other dog I came into contact with. If I could, I'd utilize my treat/belly rubs/prayer strategy. If I was without treats or opportunity, though, I'd simply crouch down and casually cover the dog's face with my hand while quickly and silently reciting a prayer that I assumed was green-lit by God: "Dear God, forgive this good boy/good girl of their sins and come into their heart and live so that they can spend eternity with you in paradise. Amen."

All the while, I would pretend to be scratching the dog's head or rubbing his neck. If you knew me as a kid and had a dog, chances are beyond absolute that I converted your dog to Christianity.[13]

I think you know this by now, but it bears repeating. I was a weird kid.

As an adult, I'm still evangelical, but just about different things. I'm pretty vigilant about flashing my lights at oncoming cars if I've just passed a hidden cop car, and I tell everyone I know about new movies, TV shows, or podcasts I listen to. That makes me sound

---

12. This was a long process. By my conservative estimations, I led Elway to the Lord more than eighty-five times.

13. My sincerest apologies if your family belonged to a different religion.

like the worst Christian, doesn't it? And I probably am. In a global game of Christianity, I would probably be one of the last selections.

I'll admit it: I was way more motivated to save dog souls as a kid than I am to save human souls now as an adult, mostly because the idea of salvation is much more nuanced to me now. At least for me, it isn't the simplistic binary of hell versus heaven anymore. And even more, our culture is hungry for receipts; people want proof on whether Christianity is truly a faith of hope and love—or a wolf in hope and love's clothing. That's why we Christians have a serious problem if we aren't consistently demonstrating which it is through the fruit of our actions. And to me, the more insidious issue is that some of us don't even care enough to address the question—and what we're doing to cause it. Conversion shouldn't be motivated by threats of hell, shouts from a bullhorn, or the allure of dog treats; rather, it should be motivated by love and trust.

five

The Value of Eating Shorts

I have what can only be explained as a whiteboard fetish. Wait, I don't think it's an actual fetish because it's not related to something sexual. That would be insane. For me. That might not be insane to you, but I don't know your life. A whiteboard saturated with colorful thoughts neatly organized into a kind of elegant utopia of creativity might be the height of sexiness to you. That's not my specific journey, but it could be *your* journey. You do you, safe place, etc.

So let's call it a whiteboard dependency. At this point, I have eight whiteboards currently in the rotation of my everyday life. And we're not talking the small, tasteful kinds you might find at Hobby Lobby.[1] I'm talking, went-to-Lowe's-had-them-cut-industrial-sized-pieces-of-bathtubs-into-giant-eight-by-ten-whiteboard-monstrosity whiteboards.

Truthfully, I could *easily* double that number and not even blink. Some people dream of uploading their consciousness onto

---

1. I actually originally used Target as the store in this example, but I was told I was using Target too much in this book, so I switched it to Hobby Lobby. I don't even know if Hobby Lobby has whiteboards. But I know that Target does, so when you read the line connected to this footnote, know that I really meant Target.

the internet and living forever as a sort of AI-infused omnipotent being. I love that for them, but my dream is to build a house for myself that is made entirely of whiteboards.[2]

Super quick, let me run down all my whiteboard locations and what they are used for.

- **Whiteboard 1:** My home office
  Purpose: Goals and stuff. Tracking progress on projects.
  Actual Use: My kids scribble on it.
- **Whiteboards 2–5:** My work office
  Purpose: Work goals. One tracks progress on screenwriting projects, one tracks progress for my podcast work, one tracks progress for my writing work, and one is simply for life to-dos.
  Actual Use: My kids scribble on it when they come see me at work.
- **Whiteboard 6:** My closet
  Purpose: For motivational quotes designed to inspire me to overachieve each and every day.
  Actual Use: My kids scribble on it.
- **Whiteboard 7:** Our home storage space where I keep my weights
  Purpose: To track progress on the different exercises I'm doing along with the weights and sets I do each time I work out.
  Actual Use: All that . . . but just one time. Ever. I work out in there semi-regularly, but have you ever worked out? It's

---

2. Is this how hoarding starts? You're just a person in the world who doesn't know why you want seventy thousand different newspapers stacked messily in your basement and then suddenly, TLC camera people knock on your door like they are serving a search warrant and you're like, "Oh wow. I guess I do maybe give off a hoarding impression."

hard. I don't want to work out *and* use a whiteboard. That's exhausting. (My kids don't scribble on this one because they are scared of the storage space.)

- **Whiteboard 8:** My home office closet

    Purpose: To be an on-call understudy whiteboard that is prepared to perform the normal duties of a regular whiteboard at a moment's notice.

    Actual Use: My kids found it and scribbled on it. With permanent markers.

So this begs the question: Why all the whiteboards? Well, do you remember Russell Crowe's John Nash in *A Beautiful Mind*? That's me—except way less smart. He's doing advanced mathematics and I'm writing down notes about how it would be funny to name a furniture store "Sectional Healing" in a fictional story. Basically the exact same thing. I have an obsession with whiteboards because I have a lot of frantic and strange thoughts and I need places to capture them. I'm told that my Enneagram type (five)[3] leaves me obsessed by information, thus my need to arrange my life around surfaces that help me capture and retain information. The idea is, if I just have all the information, I can find definition, meaning, and eventually security.

The roots of this impulse began in my childhood in the form of to-do lists. The world I was experiencing tended to feel like an incomprehensible mess, but these lists helped me reformat what I was being taught to prioritize into something actually understandable.

---

3. And I swear to you, that will be the last time I talk about Enneagram types. As a concept, they are objectively fascinating but only to the person whose personality is being talked about. In this way, they're like your fantasy football team, your dreams, or your pet. Though very interesting to you, no one else really cares.

Whether I actually did what was on my to-do lists, I don't remember. But they were a record of my thoughts of what I should and—more memorably—should not be doing.

My first to-do list was pretty standard fare for something authored by a nine-year-old. Stuff like "Don't be loud" and "Don't pee the bed." You know, the *usual* priorities of adolescence. But the most interesting inclusion on this was an entry that said "Do NOT watch *The Simpsons*."

Do you see the capitalized letters? That's not my emphasis now. That's my nine-year-old emphasis then because I meant *business*.

You might be wondering, what would compel a child to create a what-not-to-do list and include not watching *The Simpsons* on it?

Because on a very basic level, *The Simpsons* presented as a fascinating display of the forbidden. Because I was still framed out with a degree of childlike innocence, *The Simpsons* felt like a kind of Tree of the Knowledge of Good and Evil. It was particularly appealing for two very simple reasons:

1. **It was animation.** Naturally, as a devotee of Saturday morning cartoons, I reasoned that *The Simpsons* fit into the range of shows I could watch. If it was animated, it was almost certainly a show aimed at me; but this assumption was made in a time before the golden age of adult cartoons.[4]

2. **It was culturally significant.** Combining the traditional edginess of FOX programming with the format of animation was obviously wise, given the success of the show and how it

---

4. Why is it that the addition of the word *adult* onto any phrase makes the phrase feel gross? Go ahead, try it: Adult bottled water. Adult cardboard. Adult trigonometry. Adult bounce house. See? All those words were just ruined. Except for *trigonometry* because that word was already ruined.

is still running even now. Current programming like *BoJack Horseman* and *Bob's Burgers* and others make the notion of animation being purely for kids seem quaint. But back then, it was a groundbreaking idea.

But the character of Bart Simpson did not go over well with many parents, mine included. He seemed to embody the worst of what a child could be: rebellious *and* disrespectfully rude.

Now, I want to be clear that my parents weren't snake-handling radicals. That just wasn't them. They were normal. Measured. Realistic with us and engaged in our lives. Luckily for me,[5] they weren't the *Footloose* kind of parents who wouldn't let me dance with non-Christian popular culture. All this to say, I'd had a range of experiences with TV shows, and my parents had displayed competence with what they did and did not let me watch. So they'd gathered enough equity for me to respect any line they laid down.

And so, at nine years old, because of my parents' understandable conclusions about the appropriateness of *The Simpsons*, I became *Simpsons* abstinent. But not only that, I set about making sure people knew the truth about this *Simpsons* menace. I told friends at school to avoid the show at all costs and tsk-tsked those who had chosen to eat from the tree poisoned with the influence of Bart and Homer Simpson. I was so emphatic about avoiding it that I managed to very casually bring it up to parents of my friends around the neighborhood.

---

5. I say "luckily" because even then, I was familiar with the "quality" of Christian content at the time. This was the early nineties, so the creation of Christian media wasn't really a thing yet, much less for kids. There was no *VeggieTales*, guys. We're talking about the Dark Ages of Christian content. Phillips, Craig and Dean, Michael W. Smith, and Carman were the feudal lords of the musical hellscape, and the pickings for movies or TV were pretty slim.

EXT. NEIGHBOR'S FRONT DOOR—
LATE AFTERNOON

Knox knocks on the front door. After a few moments, a parent opens the door.

PARENT

Hey Knox, are you looking for *(insert any of the neighbor kids' names)*? They are with their grandparents for the day but they should be back tomorrow.

KNOX

Actually I'm here to return this Nerf gun.

PARENT

Oh, I don't think we own any Nerf guns, actually, but thanks for checking.

(Parent begins to close the door.)

KNOX

(Places his hand on the door to prevent it from closing yet)

Very good. Before I go though, Jim, have we spoken about the dangers of the television program *The Simpsons*?

PARENT

Yes, we have. Many times. And again, I do want to remind you that I remain

uncomfortable with you calling me by
my first name.

KNOX

Great feedback, Jim. Noted. And I
knew I could count on you to remain
vigilant and fight the good fight.
Anyone who tells people to *E* his *S*'s is
someone to resist and flee from.

PARENT
(Perplexed for a moment)

E his *S*'s?

KNOX
(Looks around before leaning in and whispering)

Eat. His. Shorts.

PARENT

Right. Of course. We will be remaining
vigilant.

KNOX

I knew you would. Great talk, Jim.

To be clear, I'd never actually seen an episode of the show. And
to this day, I've probably watched fewer than four total episodes,
a very embarrassing admission for a pop culture professional to
make. But in the moment, it wasn't about the actuality of the show;

it was more about the show being under the designation of something I shouldn't be doing. Ergo, it must also be something that other people shouldn't be doing either.

The thing is, once I gained a tiny bit of autonomy in choosing what played on our TV, I realized that the show—or any kind of entertainment I'd been steered away from by my parents or the church—wasn't categorically evil. And this intrigued me, not because I had any interest in the profane, but because I was still trying to understand the world. The fact that the authorities in my life dismissed certain elements of pop culture out of hand was puzzling in a way I couldn't understand then, but is wildly obvious now. I wasn't equipped to understand that just because something wasn't categorically evil didn't mean that I was emotionally prepared to confront it. My assumption, though, was that I wasn't getting the whole story, especially from the church.

The place that was teaching me the gospel didn't seem to always be the gospel about the things that existed outside their doors. In many cases, I picked up on a smearing distrust of things only because those things didn't originate from the church or have a church-approved genesis.

Moreover, I'd accepted that TV shows or movies or books could be "bad" because I'd wanted to be "good." But I wasn't the kind of make-the-world-a-better-place good kid like Malala; I was mostly motivated by avoiding the disappointment that comes with being bad. Even as I type these words, I can imagine the unwelcome feeling I get when I've disappointed someone who matters to me. My skin gets hot, and a slow burn of shame and embarrassment sinks through me like the worst anesthetic ever.

As always, when motivations spring from a place of fear, missteps follow shortly thereafter. Consider *Frozen*'s Queen Elsa, who is terrified of the powers that make her special and lives by the motto "Conceal, don't feel." She defines herself by what not to do (because that's all she's ever been taught), and in this way, she becomes less a person and more a wintry nuclear bomb, dangerous to both herself and others. Clearly, it just doesn't work to orient our lives this way.

This is extraordinarily embarrassing, but it took me years to realize that a gay person was actually, you know, just a person with thoughts and feelings and motivations and experiences all their own that worked together to inform who they were as a person.[6] But prior to that, they were just human manifestations of this thing I'd been told was bad. Why? Because it was easier to label people with a word that allowed me to dismiss them than it was to understand their complexity.

Looking for the things we disagree with and want to dismiss is such a terrible way to look at the world. We live at the most privileged time in a privileged existence on a planet privileged with life and art and love and community, all blessed by and through God. But you seriously want to boycott Starbucks for using a Christmas cup design that says "Happy Holidays" instead of "Merry Christmas"?[7] That's what you got out of (gestures wildly around indicating that I mean everything: life, existence, creation, french fries, naps) all this?

Look, as someone who is bilingual in snark and cynicism, I can say there's something momentarily clever and cool about being dismissive and loud about what you don't like and don't approve of—but wouldn't you rather celebrate what a miracle all of this is?

---

6. It took even longer to arrive at this conclusion with Democrats.

7. The only thing whiter than a tepid boycott with qualifiers is a sorority girl wondering if she should get bangs or not. I'll never forget people wanting to boycott Disney for hosting gay pride events and then softly rescinding that boycott upon realizing that ESPN was part of Disney.

I'm arriving at this conclusion woefully later than I would like. I've done myself and many others a disservice by classifying things and people by what they weren't and not what they were: "We don't do this. We don't believe that. We shouldn't talk to them." It's easy to shine a light on what you disagree with and reject; even now I could fill a whiteboard with a list of don'ts instead of dos. But I'm doing my best to say "*E* my *S*" to that attitude, even if I still feel a bit of shame that I'm quoting that noted heathen Bart when I do so.

six

Alex vs. Pat

Self-discovery is a wonderful thing. It gives you a kind of profound clarity about yourself, but it can also help inform the periphery of your worldview, specifically in regard to really arbitrary trivial things. For example, there are certain things I've come to believe are absolutely, unquestionably, universally true.

- A good sandwich can solve most problems.
- Selfies actually aren't all that bad.
- There's no socially graceful way to eat corn on the cob.
- LeBron James is better than Michael Jordan.
- Sweet potato fries are a culinary consolation prize.
- No one enjoys a drum solo. Not even the drummer doing it.
- Blanche Devereaux is the best Golden Girl and it isn't really a close call.
- The universe manifested Bradley Cooper to have the career Ryan Reynolds could not.

But one specific universal truth best communicates how I see the world: You are either a Pat Sajak kind of person or an Alex Trebek kind of person.

There's no in-between on whether you are a Sajakian or a Trebekian. No wiggle room. This isn't a BuzzFeed quiz situation where you can manipulate the answers to make yourself most like Zack from *Saved by the Bell* or Monica from *Friends*.

People, we are living in a wonderful time when conventions and institutions are being challenged and patriarchies are being toppled and you can eat breakfast at any time of the day. "Breakfast for dinner" is no longer an indictment of unpreparedness; it's a *preference*. But fundamentally, regardless of age, race, or gender, baked into our DNA is the fact that we are all either a Trebekian or a Sajakian.

Before we get to the differences between these two classifications, allow me to provide some personal context to set the larger framework. For most of early adolescence, my bedtime was 8:00 p.m. Later, when I began fourth grade, it shifted to 9:00 p.m. Now, in the big scheme of things, the difference between those bedtimes isn't much, right? It's sixty minutes. Three thousand and six hundred seconds. But the significance I want to examine here wasn't as much the length of time as it was what transpired because of this somewhat arbitrary parental decision.

To this point, going to bed at 8:00 p.m. eastern standard time meant going to bed before all the primetime TV. Was it the end of the world? No. But it did leave me knowing that just beyond the horizon of my bedtime was a kind of Narnia for situational comedies and one-liners. Instead of must-see TV like *The Cosby Show* or *A Different World* forming the infrastructure of my pop-cultural sensibilities, though, it was *Wheel of Fortune* and *Jeopardy!*

However, all was not lost for me with my 8:00 p.m. bedtime, as both *Wheel* and *Jeopardy!* still contained their own worlds of intrigue—even if not as rich as the shows existing just beyond the veil of my adolescent curfew.[1] The most intriguing detail was their ability to be similar yet diametrically opposed. They were game shows, but both went about their business very differently.

When I watched *Wheel of Fortune*, I understood the premise. I enjoyed the mystery of each puzzle. The lighting and colors were great, and the randomness and whirring of the wheel was a particular delight. And let's not even mention the strange feelings and impulses Miss Vanna White provoked. But that's where the charitable evaluations ended for me, because I could not for the life of me understand Pat Sajak.

To consider Pat Sajak is to consider the essence of modern existence. We do many things that we attach great import to. But under the surface of this self-aggrandizing lurks the need for a greater forensic reckoning as to what we're *actually* doing. In other words, there's a greater consideration begging to be studied about *how* our existence is vital and *who* it is vital to. And this gets to the core of Pat Sajak, who, as a game show host, was about as useless as the *g* in *lasagna*.

Let's consider Pat Sajak and his relationship to *Wheel of Fortune*. What does he actually do besides engage in congenial banter with the contestants?

He does not spin the wheel.[2]

He does not turn the letters.

---

1. If we're being honest, in the annals of popular culture, I think this back-to-back game show block is supremely underrated as a duo. Similar to Troy and Abed from *Community* and Brandy and Monica from "The Boy Is Mine." You know who is super overrated as a duo though? Bert and Ernie. You can't really remember which is which and they didn't even like each other.

2. While technically he does spin the wheel in the final round, this herculean effort is only expended to speed up the game, presumably so Pat can go back to spending all the money he doesn't honestly earn as host of the show.

He does not create the puzzles.

He does not produce the reward pennants that are placed on the wheel.

He does not even retrieve the prizes won by the contestants midround.

Again, more useless than nipples on the Batsuit.

Even more, the game he oversees isn't even a game of skill. It's mostly luck—luck of the spin, luck of the category, and luck of how quickly the most significant letter identifiers are deployed.

As a kid, the word *superfluous* didn't have residency in my vocabulary, but when I watched *Wheel of Fortune*, it was exemplified to me each night in the form of Patrick Leonard Sajak. To distill him down to his most base essence, he seemed like a haircut with a good suit and great smile whose efforts were perpetually given too much credit and whose successes were directly tied to the superior efforts of others. In other words, very much like the wizard from *The Wizard of Oz* or Peyton Manning on the 2015 Denver Broncos.

Which is why the contrasting vision of Pat Sajak's counterpart on *Jeopardy!* was so jarring. Alex Trebek contained multitudes. I know there's no inherent value in what I'm about to type as it's all hearsay—but it's my hearsay, so it stays:

- Alex Trebek seems like the real person the Most Interesting Man in the World from the Dos Equis commercials was based on.
- He seems like the guy who punched your dad out at the Burger King when you were a kid—but only because your dad was out of line.
- He looks like a noble Roman senator whose goodness is

such that he ultimately gets assassinated by his nefarious counterparts.

- He looks like a judge at a dog show whom you actually respect and subconsciously want to impress.
- He seems like the guy in your subdivision whose yard won Yard of the Month. For the last five years. Straight.

Trebek's game was intellectual wizardry, and he was the alpha and omega of his arena. No one else ran the show. Nobody read any cards for him. He set the terms for his game and the contestants complied, hoping and praying that their brains could respect the academic construct that Trebek thoughtfully deployed from 7:30 to 8:00 p.m. each night.

There was risk, variability, and strategy involved; and the central spoke in the show's wheel wasn't a literal wheel. It was knowledge. Something that, as a child, I intensely craved.

To know me is to know that I cope with anxiety by trying to seize control over as much as I can. It's the most charming of attributes, I know, and it makes me an extreme joy to work with, for, or under. But the method behind this madness has always been about understanding as much as possible about as much as possible so I can control as much as possible. Not necessarily in how those things affected me, but in how I allowed myself to be affected by them.

Let's consider this more anecdotally. As a boy, I spent countless nights freaking myself out because I couldn't understand the supernatural chain of command within the universe. I knew there was God at the top of the heap, but I didn't know anything else. Who was God working for? Why did he get this gig? What were his ambitions?

So I created a rudimentary flowchart of how I assumed the universe's power dynamic worked.

I knew that the first tier was God, Jesus, and the Holy Spirit. They were the original triumvirate. Like Danny Tanner, Uncle Jesse, and Uncle Joey but way better.[3]

After that, the next tier was the pastor from our church and the pope.[4] I didn't know much about the pope, but he always dressed crazy; and as I would come to learn, people who dress crazy are either legitimately crazy or incredibly famous. I correctly assumed the latter for the pope.

The next tier belonged to Dan Rather, Tom Brokaw, and Peter Jennings because they handled all the news and necessary seriousness that came with the news. This felt pretty obvious.

The next tier was Joe Montana, Michael Jordan, and Ken Griffey Jr. because they were the best at their respective sports, which had to translate to an importance commensurate with their athletic prowess.

The final tier was my parents and all the other parents of my friends because they were the local, day-to-day authorities of life.

As a kid, this all felt bulletproof logically. I may have been off by a detail or two, but this felt mostly right.

But postbedtime problems arose whenever I allowed my mind to wander to who was one rung up the chain of command from God.

---

3. I'm not sure who is who in this equation. Danny is probably the Godhead. From there, it gets murky. I'm going to say Uncle Jesse is Jesus just because of similar names and hair games. Which makes Uncle Joey the Holy Spirit? Let's just go with it.

4. RIP Pastor Bell. He was a great pastor, had a flair for the dramatic, and always called my parents by the wrong names when he greeted them by the door every Sunday. Respect.

INT. LIVING ROOM—POST BEDTIME

ME

Mom, Dad?

MOM and DAD

What?

ME

Who came before God?

MOM

(Exasperated sigh, as if to say, "This again?")

DAD

Nobody. It's just always been God. Good night.

ME

Right. Sure. But . . . how did God get here?

MOM

(Exasperated sighing)

DAD

That's the thing with God. He's infinite so he has always been here and always will be here. Good night.

ME

Of course. Obviously. But that means
he didn't have a God-mom or a God-dad?

MOM

(*Exasperatedest sighing*) Maybe he did
but he asked them too many questions
after bedtime so they left. Good night.

Going down this path of thought always provoked anxiety because I couldn't understand infinity, and I definitely could not understand God's existence. It was antithetical to everything I'd learned about life up to that point because every other question had a mostly tidy resolution.

Q: "Why do I have to eat vegetables?"
A: "Because they are healthy for you."

Q: "Why are there so many more pictures of my older sister than me?"
A: "Because the excitement of having a kid had worn off."

Q: "Why is Donald Duck always so mad?"
A: "Because Mickey Mouse has systematically marginalized him from the clubhouse and Donald may suffer from undiagnosed PTSD."

While I was learning that cause and effect could explain pretty much every question I had, I was hit with this whole God quandary where suddenly logic and reason couldn't crack the code. Seemingly, God was the puzzle no one could solve, and yet this indecipherability was super casual for everyone, like a slap bracelet for the soul.

Which is why I was a Trebekian. Sure, *Jeopardy!* wasn't about solving the mysteries and motivations of the universe, but it felt adjacent to that pursuit. In retrospect, I realize *Jeopardy!* is probably less a pursuit of intellectualism and more a formal celebration of granular trivia and the entertainment value of extraneous information—but as a kid, the dividing lines seemed starker and more important.

This need for formality, answers, and processes in the pursuit of understanding is why I was and always will be a Trebekian. It's why I couldn't just spin a wheel and see what happened. I had to understand the wheel, why it spun, and what all the spinning was really about.

But I didn't yet know that figuring out the daily doubles or mastering the wheel still wouldn't explain everything about the infinite and divine. We try to convince ourselves that we can think our way to more perfectly understanding God. We believe in our ability to accumulate clues that will help us hack our way into better standing with him. But we can't reverse engineer God by phrasing our answers in the form of a question or buying vowels. In a universe full of masterstrokes, that does feel like God's most primo masterstroke of all: that neither the Sajaks nor the Trebeks of the world can solve the supernatural puzzle that is the essence of God.

seven

The Can't-Miss Kid

When I was born, I was the subject of two distinct but wildly divergent prophecies:

- My paternal grandmother predicted that I would attend Oral Roberts University and become a great pastor in the church. (Status: This has not come to fruition. Yet. JK, that's definitely never coming to fruition.)
- My pediatrician, upon meeting newborn me, said that due to my unique name, I was destined to become the next great University of Georgia quarterback. Which is the kind of strange thing that only a Georgia fan can say. They produce great quarterbacks like the *Transformer* movies produce developed female characters.[1] (Status: This supremely has not come to fruition either.)

Absurdity aside, these two prophecies are a microcosm of the nuanced heritage of my homeland, the South.

---

1. Which makes Matt Stafford akin to Megan Fox in this scenario, and I'm pretty great with that parallel.

Alongside giving disproportionate respect to carnival food and being unable to understand why continuing to fly the Confederate flag is a terrible idea, sports and sanctification are close siblings at the tippy top of the Southern caste system.

Generally, regional greatness is derived or achieved in connection to one of those enduring institutions. So, very early, I felt these two tongue-in-cheek prophecies embedded into the subtext of who I was and who I should want to become. I didn't yet fully grasp the concept of identity, but I knew it probably needed to be found in these two areas.

So that's how I began life—with two parallel tracks to my development. I was less a person and more a measurement of proximity to these original prophecies and the priorities they asserted. Which is why at twelve years old, I made what I now realize to be a self-indulgent forerunner of what white, affluent women call a vision board.

CONTENTS OF VISION BOARD

1. Lots of pictures of me playing baseball.
2. Pilfered headlines from *Sports Illustrated* cut and clipped to where they seemed to apply to my amateur athletic exploits. (Headline appropriation, if you will.)
3. Miscellaneous athletic trinkets associated with important athletic moments. (Medals, trophies, etc.)
4. Pictures of other athletes I admired, including but not limited to:

   a. Charlie Ward
   b. Barry Larkin
   c. Ryne Sandberg

    d. Reggie White

    e. Pete Sampras

    f. Pete Sampras's bushy eyebrows

    g. John Elway

Now that I'm typing this, I'm realizing that it's heavy on the sporting emphasis. Which is a fair reflection of my priorities throughout my childhood and adolescence, but also it's because church didn't give me a commoditized industry to idolize. Which is probably wise. Posters with Joel Osteen posed heroically or Max Lucado bobbleheads would probably be a bad look.[2]

The centerpiece of my monument to youthful arrogance was the clipped headline from a *Sports Illustrated* article about Notre Dame quarterback Ron Powlus, who was called "the Can't-Miss Kid." For background, Ron Powlus was a quarterback phenom who was predicted to not just win a single Heisman but multiple Heismans while at Notre Dame. He was the most hyped of hyped college recruits of my lifetime. For Notre Dame, he was supposed to be the quarterbacking manifestation of Touchdown Jesus. He was going to spearhead the next evolution of Notre Dame football into a new golden age for the golden domers. In other words, I was aligning myself, a bucktoothed child with a severe chili-bowl haircut, with new-age Joe Montana. Lofty? Perhaps. Ambitious? To be sure.

I kept this board on my wall, adjacent to my bed, and I looked at it every morning when I woke up and every night before I went to bed. In truth, more than twenty years later, I remember the form of the room in mostly hazy detail save for two things.

---

2. Am I little surprised that there are no Joel Osteen Fatheads out there? Sure, definitely a little but the point remains: outside of Awana, there wasn't really much in the way of Christian swag to prove how ride or die you were for God other than those W.W.J.D. bracelets.

1. That vision board.
2. A super dope papasan chair I got from Pier 1.

Whenever I think about that papasan chair, I get wistful. That chair was the Balki to my Cousin Larry, the Luigi to my Mario. It was the greatest, and it has ruined other chairs for me. At least twice a year, I'll be drinking coffee at my kitchen table and think, *You know, I should buy a papasan chair.* For some people, it's a boat or a beach house or a timeshare in Boca. But for me, it's the sweet plushy bliss of a papasan.

Whenever I think about that vision board, though, I feel a ton of shame. Not the kind of shame where you feel like you've done a terrible, godless thing. Rather the kind specifically associated with hubris gone awry, like when Garth Brooks had his whole Chris Gaines experiment.[3] Just, "What was I thinking?"

I often wonder what my family must have thought about my board. We've never talked about this physical shrine, but I'm sure they assumed they were sharing a home with a burgeoning egomaniac. But it wasn't that I necessarily thought I was this incredible person. In truth, I've always been hypervigilant about two things:

1. **Not having bad breath.** In middle school, I ate so many peppermints in fear of having bad breath that I ruined my teeth beyond repair. They aren't ugly or anything, but you know when there is just an inherent sense that the vibe is unsustainable? That's my teeth. Like Britney Spears in 2007 but more enamel based.

---

3. Do you think he ever talks about that? Do you think his closest friends ever dare to broach that whole phase, or do they all know it to be the Bad Idea We Must Never Speak Of?

2. **Not appearing arrogant.** This somehow adversely implies that I have plenty of things to be arrogant about. I don't. I'm pretty much your average white guy from the South. Most of my date nights with Ashley end with us at Target, some of my relatives have been to jail, and I get overly emotional about football. For a few years in elementary school, I thought my thumbs were double-jointed[4] and I could tend to get a little uppity about it, but other than that, I'm pretty basic.

Really, I was vigilant about this because early on, I could tell that no one likes someone who is arrogant, even if for good reason. Arrogance is like a skunk's spray; the skunk might have had a great reason to spray, but it is still highly unpleasant.

So the board wasn't a shrine to myself. Quite the opposite. It was a shrine to what I wanted to become. What I thought my identity should be. To this point, it was my epicenter of aspiration. I wanted to be great. I wanted to be something significant because, again, as tongue-in-cheek as those prophetic expectations were, I did feel the burn of attaining something close to them. The most obvious place for this to occur was sports, but that was just the simplest way to express this idea.

It's such an audacious thing to aspire as a kid because you don't really know anything. I mean, you think you know things, like how Macho Man Randy Savage was transcendently cool and how fine dining doesn't get any finer than a McDonald's Happy Meal. But turns out, in retrospect, the Macho Man did seem to be vaguely

---

4. They weren't and remain single-jointed to this day.

misogynisty. And also McDonald's doesn't even have the best fried chicken in the fast-food game.[5]

But those things felt *very* true at the time simply because they were immediately and uniquely specific to my limited worldview. I wasn't building my life around those opinions or anything, but it would be disingenuous of me to act like I didn't have other opinions informed by experience that I *was* very much building my life around. For example:

1. **I wanted to be a professional baseball player.** Not too weird. I was aware of the odds, but I loved baseball and was reasonably good at it.
2. **I wanted to get married at Disney World.** Okay. Not weird per se, but strangely specific for a twelve-year-old boy.
3. **I wanted to make enough money as a professional baseball player that I could rent out Disney World for said wedding.** Now this is just financially impractical. Somewhere, a shiver just went down Dave Ramsey's spine.

These aspirations were the truest things in my life.[6] But my wanting these things didn't mean I knew what attaining them would cost. They just hung there in a void, orbiting my consciousness, waiting for some kind of reality to be constructed around them.

I don't think I'm breaking any new ground when I say that, to some extent, we're all born with an expectation of greatness. It's

---

5. That goes to Popeyes. Come at me on that and I will burn you to the ground. I've really thought about it, and I'm willing to get into a fistfight over this. My editors tell me I shouldn't invite people to fistfight me in the footnotes over fast-food fried chicken, but they are wrong.

6. Along with the papasan chair. Do not forget about the papasan chair.

why most kids want to be princesses or ninjas or princess ninjas or President Princess Ninja of the United States. I think we all believe that there's a capacity for greatness somewhere inside us.

And I agree with that. It might be glib and naive, but I really do believe it. As we age, I don't think this goes away; it just gets more finely tuned and appropriate. Maybe it goes from President Princess Ninja of the USA to just becoming president of an HOA who does karate on the side.[7] But whatever it is, I think we want to belong to something, and we want to be good at whatever it is we do. And those are great ideas—but they aren't an identity.

Consider this list of the biggest Can't-Miss Kids I remember from popular culture. I include them because I've always identified them primarily by their success. But when you look deeper, their successes come more into question.

- Doogie Howser, MD

  Success: He was a doctor at like ten years old. No doy.

  Why there's more to it: You think child actors have a high burnout rate? I can't even imagine child doctors. We've got kids coming unglued after filming fifty shows on the Disney Channel. What's going to happen to a kid who watches people bleed out? I mean, look at the doctor turnover on *Grey's Anatomy*. Those characters aged in dog years. And not the good dog years. Pug dog years.

- Reggie Mantle

  Success: From the *Archie* comics, Reggie is the definition of tall, dark, and handsome. His family is wealthy and

---

7. If that's you and you honestly aspire to become president of an HOA, I can only hope it's so that you can legislate that HOA into oblivion. HOAs are worse than butt cancer, man.

his father owns a media company. His main rival is a ginger named Archie whose best friend is obsessed with hamburgers.

Why there's more to it: Reggie is widely held to be the least likable character in *Archie,* and despite looks, power, and money, he can't subvert Archie as the coolest kid at Riverdale. Also, Reggie aspires to a career in comedy even though we all know that only broken people try to be funny.

- Warner from *Legally Blonde*

  Success: First, "Warner" is an expert-level white-rich-kid name. I heard that if you say "Warner" three times in front of a mirror, Mr. J.Crew from J.Crew will manifest and grant you three wishes all related to boat shoes, seersucker, or lacrosse.

  Second, he's a good-looking wannabe lawyer at Harvard.

  Third, Reese Witherspoon's Elle Woods is into him.

  Why there's more to it: Even though Elle Woods is into him, he isn't into her, which is the most unbelievable part of a movie replete with unbelievable sequences. *Legally Blonde*–era Reese Witherspoon is like Bo Jackson in *Tecmo Bowl* or Michael Vick in *Madden NFL 2004.* Just completely unstoppable. She is throwing seven different kinds of smoke, and Warner's all like, "Yeah, great, but I really want to focus on my lawyering studies right now."

  When a guy says that he just wants to focus more on his studies than be with a girl, that's a pseudo-courteous way of saying "Pass." Because, remember, men can be insane when it comes to courting ladies. Ancient dudes were so thirsty for Helen of Troy in *The Iliad* that a war was fought that led to both Eric Bana and Brad Pitt dying. All that to say, there seems to be a loose thread to Warner that if pulled, would probably reveal something very humbling.

- The kid from *The Giving Tree*

  Success: Let's talk about this jerk sandwich for a minute. So he discovers this supernatural, anthropomorphic tree who loves him and wants to give him stuff.

TREE

Hey kid. You're awesome. I love you. I just want to help you in your life for no apparent reason even though it might be destructive to me. I'll do anything you want.

KID

Yeah, yeah. That's great. How's about you gimme some more of that sweet, sweet hickory wood so I can sell it.

TREE

(*Taken aback*) Okay. Sure. Yeah. Sure thing. (*Unsteady pause*) So you wanna sell it, huh?

KID

Yup. To get money.

TREE

Okay. I guess that makes sense. So you can pay for college or something like that?

KID

Nah, so I can get an airbrushed T-shirt
for a girl I like.

TREE

(Pregnant pause. Looks around to make sure
it's not getting *Punk'd*.)

An airbrushed T-shirt? Like you can
get in Panama City?

KID

How do you know about Panama City?

TREE

I'm a magic tree. I know things.

KID

That weirdly makes sense.

TREE

I don't know. I'm not so sure this is
a good—

KID

You said anything I want.

Why there is more to it: The kid couldn't parlay this
supernatural tree into anything great. *It was a magic tree*

that spoke to him, and the only thing he was successful in was exploiting the tree into ruin. This kid is basically like the Indianapolis Colts with Andrew Luck.

Still, for all of these characters, their shorthand identity was all about success. But when I looked deeper, that definition became more complicated. And that's something I've been fascinated with ever since I realized I didn't want to become a baseball player and I didn't want to get married at Disney World. Even deeper, when I finally realized that I wasn't going to competently define myself through church or sports,[8] that's when I started attempting to understand myself.

Sports were actually pretty graceful about my realization because, by nature, they're ruthlessly efficient. You and the sport both have to opt in, and it only takes one of you to opt out. If you aren't good enough, eventually you get left behind. But even if you are, you have to continue opting in amid more work, more scrutiny, and more pressure. So no University of Georgia quarterbacking for me.

On the other hand, defining yourself through church is an entirely different thing. It's a cultural affiliation before it's even a personal one, so it's a tricky task to deconstruct what you believe versus what you've just inherited through participation. But early on, I wasn't "good" at church like others were. I was argumentative, I had a lot of questions, and I had a crippling anxiety of praying in public. All these seemed to loudly declare that I could never live up to my grandma's Oral Roberts–tinged expectations of me.

---

8. Timeline-wise, this occurred around the age of eighteen. Though I played baseball and led praise and worship, I was confronted with the respective realities that I couldn't hit a slider and my singing voice could be best described as "Pitchy, but tries really, really hard."

As an early enthusiast of vision boards and a person who had dueling prophecies foisted upon his name, I can say authoritatively that there's nothing more futile than trying to force expectations to become your reality. My assumption that I would only find success and identity through one of those two areas limited how I experienced my life. On a different level, it limited my understanding and awareness of how I could interpret God. Since I was used to only considering the world through two lenses, that impulse informed how I allowed myself to think of God too.

But let me tell you, there's something beautiful about finding God in a place you weren't expecting. This is especially so when you've developed a sense of fatigue and discontentedness with the normal ways you expected to or were allowed to experience God. Maybe *beautiful* isn't the word. Maybe *poignant* is better. Perhaps even *cathartic*, because anytime it happens for me, there's the dual power of the experience of God in the way you aren't prepared for, but even more, I'm reminded that God exists beyond borders and designations. He's just God like that, despite my attempts to limit him to only on Sundays and only in books within the Christian Living section at various bookstores.

Recently I've been watching and rewatching the movie *Moana* with my kids. We watch it in the way all small kids like to watch a movie into the ground. To briefly summarize, *Moana* is, surprise, the story of Moana, a girl born to an island community who is destined for *something*. What that something is, she kind of knows, but she has almost no idea about how she will pursue that something. I didn't go into watching this movie expecting to identify with a teenage Polynesian princess, but not knowing how to pursue that thing you feel so strongly about is kind of my thing.

The only thing routinely buoying Moana in this belief is the ocean. The ocean is portrayed as a mystical omnipresent and omniscient character who slowly reveals itself to Moana as she needs, but never in the ways she expects. (And just as a sidenote, for me, there is an extreme amount of church in the last part of the previous sentence.)

Early in the movie, Moana is a little girl who has already managed to internalize a fear of the ocean that her community is built around, but the water attempts to connect with her after she cares for a tiny sea turtle. First, the water pulls back its tide and reveals a beautiful seashell, which she inspects and collects. It shows her several more as it coaxes her into walking farther into a pulled-back portion of the sea, revealing a snippet of a glorious and beautiful vision of the ocean and perhaps a vague promise of the things to come for her life, before returning her back to the shore for her father to find her. It is not hyperbole when I say that I cry during this scene every time. I'm a little teary right now just thinking of it because the idea behind it is so affecting to me.

Why? For most of my believing life, God has been this preexisting curriculum I had to get up to speed with, which I couldn't question or doubt. Every connection to him just felt immensely complicated and cloaked in an abrasive formality. But, to me, this scene is about God and the simplicity within which he can sometimes exist. That's not meant as a minimization of God, rather a confession that I've participated in a vast conspiracy to complicate God and assign motivation to him that only functions to disguise his truest essence. In doing this, I've layered him with a pastiche of complexity all of my own doing. But when I think of that scene from *Moana*, it makes me wonder: Is it possible that there's a simplicity to the complexity of God? Is it possible that the God I learned about in the Old Testament, who could level cities with fire and order the firstborn children of Egypt dead because of a national stalemate—could it be that his real nature is like the patient and benevolent water in *Moana*?

The idea of a supernatural force revealing itself to me when I need it but never how I expect? I resonate with this notion of God so hard that it probably registers on the Richter scale. And if I can understand a little better who God is, maybe I can understand a little more clearly who he meant me to be.

eight

The Seven Suspected Antichrists

The part I miss most about childhood is how full of mystery it all is. Growing up is as full of mystery as Magnum PI's closet is full of Hawaiian shirts. Truly just an embarrassment of mysterious riches, and nothing but time and opportunity to wonder about what it all means. And the even better part is by "it all" I don't mean anything that profound or intellectually disorienting. I spent hours wondering about the answers to questions like:

- How does the light in the fridge know when to come on?
- Why does the "pink stuff" medicine taste so good?
- Why is no one weirded out by how Scooby-Doo can talk and eat six-foot hoagies in one gulp?

But of all the mysteries out there, three reigned supreme in captivating my attention:

1. What was Carmen Sandiego's deal?
2. What was so great about Waldo?
3. Who was the Antichrist?

Now, I realize one of those mysteries greatly differs from the others, but let's go in order.

Carmen Sandiego had a backstory and a bio, but I wasn't buying any of it. Frankly, no one else was either. You didn't have to be a gumshoe to see the flimsiness of the explanation we were getting about her.

For me, it kept coming back to her being so attractive. In my limited experience of watching and perceiving heroes and villains, villains were mostly ugly or characterized with very unfortunate affectations like wispy mustaches or scars. But Carmen was pretty smoking, so this confused me. Why would she resort to international espionage and thievery? It made no sense.

The most obvious explanation to me was that Carmen was actually a rogue agent trying to uncover something untoward. Complicating this was the fact that the Chief and Rockapella were invested in ensuring her silence, and thus they made us, the viewers and contestants, complicit in achieving that end. Because, really, who seemed more untrustworthy: Carmen Sandiego, a secret agent with supermodel-level hotness *or* the five grown dudes who have built a life making instrument noises with their mouths? It's pretty much spelled out right there.

Conversely, the mystery around Waldo was grounded less in him and more in the hubbub constructed *around* him. He was distinctly dressed and traveled a lot, but other than that, what evidence were we given that we should be fixated on finding this guy? Everyone is tough to pick out of a crowd. Again, it smelled like a conspiracy to me. Who was funding all his travel? What was Waldo distracting us from noticing? Classic Trojan horse, that Waldo.

But the mystery around the identity of the Antichrist leveled things up significantly. We weren't talking about mysteries limited to fictional universes; we were talking about the very real Son of Perdition, the actual opposite of Jesus Christ. The incarnation of evil.

Frankly, this mystery threatened to consume my life because... how could it not? The Antichrist was the person who would launch the world into a physical and spiritual Tribulation that would then give way to Arma-freaking-geddon.

I wish I could appropriately convey to you how large the idea of Armageddon and the Antichrist loomed over everything. This mystery and the fear and dread of hell were the two things I thought about probably more than anything else throughout my childhood. To say that my fearful fascination with hell and the Antichrist informed and motivated much of who I was and much of who I came to be is the most understated of understatements. Terror and urgency motivated me, so, as I was wont, I leveraged popular culture in an effort to understand this preeminent supernatural battle. I thought that if that was how I made sense of the world and myself, maybe it could also help with this whole Antichrist thing?

I never realized it until now, but it's funny how much I refused to "lean not" on my own understanding, as Proverbs so routinely told me to. I don't think it was a matter of disobedience as much as it was about not understanding how someone could lean on anything beyond their own understanding. My own understanding was the only understanding I could access. How else is a kid supposed to interpret the world except through what he is familiar with?

In an effort to solve the Antichrist mystery, I read all of Hal

Lindsey's books[1] and any other apocalyptically tinged paperbacks I could get my hands on, which was, surprisingly, not a lot.

Which was another mystery. I didn't understand why more people weren't consumed by this like I was. It was a layered cake of crazy events, such as people being instantaneously raptured into heaven, a superhuman man-devil taking control of the world, and Jesus coming back like Rocky Balboa to pound this Ivan Drago-esque superdemon into the lake of fire. I'm being very serious when I say that this seemed like the only story that mattered. At the time of the apex of this fascination, I was aware that Bill Clinton had made some very poor decisions about remembering he was married and that O. J. Simpson had made some even poorer decisions,[2] but those felt much more like "Meanwhile, back at the ranch" moments to the more important story concerning the impending apocalypse. I just could not let it go.

I remember interrupting my youth minister to pepper him with questions during a Disciple Now study[3] as he made an impassioned plea about salvation.

INT. DISCIPLE NOW—EVENING

Youth pastor is in earnest prayer. All the students have their heads bowed in similar earnestness, except for Knox. He's approaching the front of the stage like he's the neighbor

---

1. If you don't know who Hal Lindsey is, he's an evangelist and a prolific author of end-times literature. Also, he looks like if Lee Corso from ESPN's *College GameDay* had a little more hair and the mustache of a villain.

2. Allegedly. LOL.

3. These were youth group weekends where you and your other same-aged-and-gendered peers would stay at a host home and do various youth group activities all related to the Bible and discipleship. Lit level: extreme.

who wants to remind you to keep your dog off his grass.

YOUTH PASTOR

. . . and it's not about hell, it's about the hope and freedom in Christ. So if you're here tonight and—

KNOX

Excuse me! Really quick. I love everything you are talking about. But I do have a very quick question about the nature of the Antichrist—

YOUTH PASTOR

But I'm praying right now. We're all praying right now. Do you see everyone and how they are bowing their heads and closing their eyes?

KNOX

(Knox looks around and recognizes this.)

I do. Totally. I get that. I do. But I just feel like as a youth group we're not talking *enough* about Antichrist awareness, do you know what I mean? Do you ever get that sense?

YOUTH PASTOR

Can we talk about this later?

KNOX

Right, *but*, what if later is too late?

YOUTH PASTOR

It won't be.

KNOX

But how do you . . .

YOUTH PASTOR

(To himself, quietly)

Dear Jesus, give me patience.

KNOX

Are you praying to God right now? Can
you ask him my question? He might
listen more to you. I'll wait here and
just listen.

The whole thing bamboozled me. I wanted to know: Was being
the Antichrist like wearing the yellow jersey during the Tour de
France in that it was a status to be opted into, *or* was someone born
expressly to be the Antichrist? Because, to be honest, that seemed
like extraordinarily bad luck. Can you imagine living your life and
making plans and then getting the call that actually you are to be
the Demon Supreme that will initiate the end of all things? That's
rough, man. I always felt bad for the drummer who left Hootie & the
Blowfish to become a youth pastor right before they became huge,

but I felt even worse for the person who would be conscripted into demonic villainy.

Luckily for me, the Left Behind books came out to help assuage my curiosity. Written by Tim LaHaye and Jerry B. Jenkins, these midnineties books were speculative fiction about what will happen at the end of the world, all centered around a cast of ne'er-do-wells turned Christian heroes. In the books, these newly saved protagonists were tasked with contending with a world overrun with tribulation and the ascendant Antichrist named Nicolae Carpathia. And all of it was (chef's kiss) storytelling manna to my curious twelve-year-old mind.

Also, can I just give shoutouts to Tim LaHaye and Jerry Jenkins for the name "Nicolae Carpathia"? Those books have a lot of issues, but their naming of the Antichrist is perfection. It did have the unintended consequence of turning an entire generation of readers from the American South against any moderately attractive European man for fear that he was the camouflaged Antichrist. I'm serious—if you are from the South and read those books and don't find yourself being intensely skeptical of Ralph Fiennes, Jude Law, and Daniel Craig, you are a trillion percent lying.

But for me, this didn't really matter because I knew this characterization of the Antichrist was faulty from the jump. If you were paying attention at all, you knew that the eventual Antichrist wouldn't be some wealthy Mediterranean shipping magnate with a billion dollars and a jawline you could build a life around; he was going to be someone we knew. Partially because we were becoming more and more globalized, but also because everything I read said so. The paperback speculations I read didn't talk about unknown entities; they zeroed in on famous people, which is what

I did as I cobbled my own short list for who I suspected to be the Wicked One. I became a sort of Harriet the Spy, but instead of consuming tomato sandwiches and training for life as a sleuth, I was consuming books about Armageddon and training my mind to be able to spot who would be at the center of this battle for all time. Sometimes I would find the clues, sometimes they would find me, but I was playing the long game. It was a list in progress. It wasn't bound by time or space or by a physical notebook; it existed in my head, and I was always adding to it, even into my college years.

They say a good collegiate athletic director always has a piece of paper listing the five coaches he would try to hire if his current one left. Well, that was me, but with the Antichrist.

As such, here are some of the most promising Antichrist candidates I collected over the years.

Tiger Woods

Reasons Tiger Woods Might Be the Antichrist
1. He seemed to make certain[4] kinds of white people really, really mad.
2. He was incredible at a sport that most people didn't care about, which was a genius move. Being incredible at baseball, basketball, football, or soccer would garner tons of acclaim and scrutiny. But golf? Golf is a sport that goes to great lengths to make you *not* want to play it.

    I hesitate to describe golfers and people who work at

---

4. Read: "the stupid kind."

golf courses this way, but they all tend to act like you've just insulted them on their Facebook walls. So to me, if Tiger were the Antichrist, this would have been a great cover. Everyone around him would have been arguing about pace of play and whether hybrid clubs are unnatural, and they totally would have missed him consolidating his power base for Antichristery.

Current Antichrist Likelihood: Highly unlikely

A sex scandal pre-Armageddon seems very counterintuitive. Also, his body can't handle golf anymore, so how are we supposed to buy him as someone who wants to go toe-to-toe with Jesus?

Peyton Manning

Reasons Peyton Manning Might Be the Antichrist

1. At one point, he was well on his way to becoming the greatest quarterback in the history of ever, which would have been a great power base of respect from which to operate.[5]
2. His omnipresence as a pitchman in commercials seemed like a great opportunity to normalize his Antichristness and work in some subliminal messages. "Better Ingredients, Better Pizza . . . Better New World Order ushered in by me, the Abomination of Desolation."
3. He has a gigantic forehead that I could only assume was that large because it was keeping so many Antichrist secrets.

---

5. But then Tom Brady happened.

Current Antichrist Likelihood: Unlikely

Like Tiger's, Peyton's body broke down. But he does have a penchant for coming up short in big moments, which would fall in line with his prophesied failure against Jesus in Armageddon. Basically what I'm saying is that if Peyton Manning were the Antichrist, and Jesus came down from heaven in a Florida Gators jersey, Armageddon would be a beatdown.

Bill Gates

Reasons Bill Gates Might Be the Antichrist

1. Super-duper, stupid rich.
2. Cornered the computer market and was probably the guy who would be responsible for implanting everyone with tiny computer chips, which would then become the mark of the Beast.
3. Was responsible for Clippit, the personified paperclip that accosted you anytime you wanted to create a document in Windows circa 1997 to 2004. Quintessence of evil.

Current Antichrist Likelihood: Unlikely

Still super-duper, stupid rich, but he's devoted himself to numerous humanitarian causes. Also, if he were going to go into Antichrist mode, it feels like he would have done it by now.

Tom Cruise

Reasons Tom Cruise Might Be the Antichrist

1. Famous and popular actor.

2. He had a bizarre New Age feel to him even before the Scientology stuff came out.

Current Antichrist Likelihood: Unlikely

Tom Cruise definitely looks the part and seemingly hasn't aged in twenty years, which *could* be indicative of some kind of satanic pact. But his candidacy does take a hit given how spectacularly he was curbed by Katie Holmes.

Marilyn Manson

Reasons Marilyn Manson Might Be the Antichrist

1. He seems like he wants it so bad, and, on some level, he needs people like me to consider it.
2. Understand, this felt super on the nose at the time, but he was really leaning into it. Personally, I have higher expectations for the Antichrist. I need him to be more suave. Like, I could see him tricking me into becoming his minion. It wouldn't be likely, but it also wouldn't be the craziest thing in the world.

Current Antichrist Likelihood: Extremely not very

He's just so thirsty to be the Antichrist that the desperation is unbecoming for the would-be Destroyer of Nations. Also, he's generally not compelling. If I don't even want to hear his music, why would I want to spend eternity with him?

Ryan Seacrest

Reasons Ryan Seacrest Might Be the Antichrist

1. He's so smooth, and I just want to trust everything he says.

2. He always deftly manages *American Idol* results and contestants. This is a guy used to dealing with many different agendas and making people feel heard, which is an especially valuable skill when considering how the Antichrist is going to have to unite contentious religions, regions, and demographics like vegans versus nonvegans.

3. Between his radio show and his spot on *Live with Kelly and Ryan,* he has his finger on the pulse of the culture as well as a mouthpiece to influence it.

4. Not only that, he may be responsible for destabilizing culture as the executive producer responsible for foisting *Keeping Up with the Kardashians* upon us.

5. He did have some allegations directed at him in 2017 and early 2018 that suggested sexual malfeasance in the workplace, which does remind me of the power-dynamic manipulations Nicolae Carpathia used on Hattie Durham in the original *Left Behind* book.

Current Antichrist Likelihood: MEGA-LIKELY

The only counterargument to Seacrest being the Antichrist is that it does seem like he uses a lot of self-tanner and, frankly, naturally glowing skin seems like something the Antichrist would just already have?

Jonathan Taylor Thomas

Reasons JTT Might Be the Antichrist
1. That hair.
2. That skin.

3. That incredibly catchy initial shorthand "JTT."
4. The fact that he was Simba in *The Lion King.*
5. The fact that multiple generations of women still have a connection to him.

Current Antichrist Likelihood: NEAR CERTAINTY

Granted, he has been off the radar for a while outside of some directing, but the question is, *why* has he been off the radar? Pursuing his artistic interests? Pursuing education? *Or perhaps laying the foundation for his Antichrist-ness?*

Obviously this list remains fluid, but I realize now that this impulse to pin down the Antichrist was a grotesque mutation of faith. The dread of judgment, the violence of the Old Testament, and the us-versus-them mentality I inherited as a Bible Belt Christian in the eighties and nineties immeasurably influenced how I understood the book of Revelation as well as the anxiety I felt as I tried and failed to identify who this Antichrist fella would be. Making peace with the idea that certain aspects of God are unknowable felt very natural to my faith. But the unsolved mystery about Satan's minion? I didn't need Robert Stack to emphasize how unsettling that was.

But that's the thing; as kids, in life, faith, and other mysteries, we're much more comfortable with just letting the mystery be, but way less so as adults. Even now, as a married guy with kids, I'm still chasing down some kind of understanding of both the big and small questions of life. But now especially, I have to fight the impulse to lean on my own understanding instead of trusting that God's got this, whatever "this" might be.

It's difficult to not want to lean on my own understanding because the questions now at my age come at an intersection of wonder and fear. The mystery about what things mean and the fear of never being able to understand them.

There's a cheesy cliché you've probably heard: "Not all who wander are lost." But the truth is, not all who wonder are lost either. I like that because it gives me room to be specifically uncertain within a larger, faithful certainty.

nine

The Sexy Car Wash

When I was eleven, I saw my first pornographic movie. I don't even think my mom knows this, and we certainly have never had a conversation about the occasion of my first porno, so let's all give my mom a second to bounce back from the existential dread she's most certainly feeling right now. I'm a parent, and I can't imagine the feeling of finding out that one of my kids has chosen to write about their first experience with a porno in a book. Thoughts and prayers for my mom right now, guys.

I was pretty sheltered as a kid. My parents' childhood experience came with a, shall we say, more laissez-faire parenting approach, which was the way of their parents' generation. But as we know because of science things, every parental philosophy provokes an equal and opposite parental philosophy. As such, my parents opted for a more involved role in the everyday life of me and my sister.

Choosing a parenting strategy, in general, is tough, because you have to look at the long-term effects and unintended consequences of whatever approach you choose.

Is it better to limit your kids and make things pretty conservative in the early going? Maybe, but then does that virtually assure that they will get neck tattoos, experiment with every illegal substance under the sun, and star in multiple seasons of *The Bachelor* and/or *Bachelorette* franchise as "the wildcard" contestant who will do anything, anywhere, with anyone? Who can say for sure? Conversely, do you let them watch horror movies at age six, drink wine by age eight, and let them host Caligula-inspired unchaperoned sleepovers with potential love interests throughout their teenage years? Again, guys, I'm not an expert.

I do give props to my parents' strategy because, in the words of Dave Matthews, you can always hike up the skirt of life a little more, but you can't hike it down. If you let your eight-year-old watch *Game of Thrones*, I'm not going to judge you. But just know that *Moana* or *Frozen* just won't have the same kind of giddy-up once they've seen Khaleesi in sexual congress with the King in the North.

I know this isn't a parenting book, but I will say that for my specific personality, the sheltering tactic was good. I was deeply impressionable, so I don't know what would have happened if I would have been exposed to both the execution and concept behind Madonna's "Like a Virgin" at a very young age, but it probably would not have been good. The butterfly effect of growing up under this parenting strategy, though, is that when you do have your first collision with something outside the sheltering umbrella, it can be extremely jarring. Let's examine just such an occasion.

I'd been invited to a sleepover with an older kid I played with on a sports team,[1] so this was a pretty choice social development for me. I went over to his house, and we did pretty standard boy

---

1. I'm being purposefully vague so I don't out this person, but know that it pains me *greatly* to speak in the syntax of someone who says things like, "That guy out there slam-dunked a real doozy of a home touchdown run!" It hurts, but I'm no snitch.

stuff—jumping on the trampoline, eating pizza, playing video games, and making fart noises, both fictional and nonfictional, with our various orifices. You know, all the usual things.

After a raucous game of wiffle ball Home Run Derby, my friend and I headed to a fence leading to a wide-open expanse of land— and he produced a heretofore unseen gun. I've thought about this memory a lot, and I still have no idea where the gun came from. Did he have a hidden compartment? Did he have it tucked in his pants the entire time we were playing Home Run Derby, like some kind of wiffle ball Johnny Utah?

Now, it's important to know that throughout my childhood, my mom often repeated three mantras to me. These weren't Bible verses, motivational sayings, or famous quotes; they were just the things she wanted to emphatically remind me that she would not be doing in the event of my poor decision-making.

- If I ever had that twinkle in my eye making her think that I might be considering premarital sex: "Just remember, your father and I won't raise a child born out of wedlock. *You* get that privilege."
- In case she saw me noticing beer commercials with a consideration that suggested future dabblings in the alcohols: "Don't forget, your dad and I won't pay for rehab."
- And lastly, on the off chance that I was showing a growing interest in firearms: "Remember: if you shoot yourself, we aren't paying for whatever body part you shot off."

My mom said a great many other things to me over the course of my childhood. Some funny, some poignant, some lovely, and some hilarious. But these were the statements that stuck with me the most.

To her credit, they worked. I had no children out of wedlock, I have never been to rehab, and I haven't yet shot off a part of my body.[2]

Luckily for my mom, I wasn't that interested in guns, despite the fact that owning firearms is a cultural norm in the South. I just didn't care for them in general, but also because I was traumatized by the *90210* episode when David Silver's friend, Scott, accidentally shot himself at a party and died. Scott was trying to be an awesome teenager and twirl a gun on his finger like he was a gunslinger, but instead he blew a giant hole in his chest, bled out, and really submarined the vibe of the party.[3] Gone, but not forgotten, Scott (RIP).

Anyway, my friend raised said gun, leveled his aim at a clearing twenty or thirty yards away, and fired a few shots toward a standing tier of glass bottles. I remember him hitting a few bottles and then handing the gun to me, which I took, but probably as awkwardly as possible.[4] In effect, the gun felt like holding a lightsaber— awe-inspiring but also almost certainly the instrument of my demise. In retrospect, the gun itself was probably a small, generic handgun, but at the time I treated it like it was a combination of Al Capone's tommy gun, Dirty Harry's revolver, and whatever sniper rifle Bradley Cooper used in *American Sniper* when he wasn't holding his crazily fake plastic baby.

I had a moment of dread because I'd internalized my mom's disapproval of this handheld death ray. But I also knew that explaining as much to my cooler, older friend was suboptimal.

---

2. *Yet.*

3. If you have a moment, I urge you to look up the clip of this on YouTube. This was a generationally important TV show, and this scene has the gravitas of an infomercial. It's truly incredible.

4. I'm sure that I held the gun like most men hold a box of tampons when they are asked to pick some up on their way home.

In terms of parental obedience, every decision a child makes exists against the backdrop of "obedient or disobedient" binary. But there are complicating factors. Especially when you pass into the realm of attempted hot-shottery,[5] obedience isn't just a yes-no proposition; it's more a spectrum. Which is to say that to dismiss any and all proposed hot-shottery is a surefire way to invite peer disappointment, but, even more, it assigns a sort of scarlet-lettered anti-hot-shottery sentiment upon you. The way I saw things, I was certainly free to appear anti-hot-shottery, but it just seemed easier to attempt the hot-shottery even if it meant maiming myself.[6]

So I accepted the gun into my hands and squeezed the trigger in the general direction of the standing bottles. I hit nothing. I squeezed the trigger enough to be enthusiastic, but not so much that I seemed like an overenthused psycho.

"Cool, right?" my friend asked, taking the gun back from my shaking hand. I was grateful that the gun was out of my hand because I just knew that if I held it for ten seconds more, I'd figure out a way to accidentally shoot off both of my legs. But there was a part of me that felt heightened from the experience, as though I'd collided with something unfamiliar and powerful.

The next day, my friend and I were lounging in front of the TV, taking some refuge from the midmorning sun. My friend was channel surfing, and we bounced around from *SportsCenter* to *This Week in Baseball* to a couple of game shows before landing on a straight-up, red-blooded pornographic movie.

---

5. The word I really wanted to use here rhymes with *dadbass*, but it was deemed to be too godless, which is an important qualification to make in the context of a chapter discussing a child seeing porn.

6. This is why so many teenagers make the decision to try to light their farts on fire; it's just the simpler social alternative.

Now, for some insight on me, this wasn't some Holy Grail I'd been chasing. It wasn't even a cursory interest. I suppose that sexuality and sexy things existed in some repressed compartment of my subconscious at this age, but I wasn't yet at the point where I would watch the premium cable channels and pray to God for a miraculous momentary unscrambling of an adult movie so that I might be blessed with the bounty of seeing a stray breast (even though the mechanism of my request seemed morally at odds with the request I was making). No way, friend. I was still in the primordial soup of that development process. Which is why I was less enthralled with what I was seeing and more feeling like I was being firehosed in the face with some kind of unrequested sex cannon.

I wasn't stupid. I understood what I was seeing, and I'd certainly been aware of sexuality prior to that moment. But until then, it was almost like I'd been taking sips of awareness and understanding, and suddenly I was confronted with a tsunami of visuals about what I had been circling.

Again, I cannot emphasize enough how casual all this was. It was the L. L. Bean of pornographic situations, comfortable *and* casual, except it was not comfortable for me because I was almost hyperventilating out of fear. I was sure that at any moment, the morality police were going to bust in like marines and hustle me off to eternal solitary confinement with only Precious Moments figurines and Thomas Kinkade paintings to keep me company.

All this was complicated by my logistical confusion about the "movie"—and I use the sarcastic air quotes around the word *movie* because, though I was young, I'd seen enough movies to know that this was a movie in the same way Danny DeVito and Arnold Schwarzenegger are twins in the 1988 movie *Twins*: technically, I guess, but not in the spirit of the idea. The context for the sexiness was actual car washing. I remember thinking that what they were doing was not an effective method for washing the car. I'd had several years of car-washing reps under my belt, and none of them were remotely sexy. In fact, they were kind of stressful because you had to do the soap, but then also wash the soap off before it started to dry on the car paint—and none of the people in the movie seemed aware of that compressed timeline. Frankly, their cavalier behavior about the cleanliness of the vehicle upon which they fornicated was very distressing to me.

I was registering what was on the screen, but I wasn't entirely processing it. You know how in *The Little Mermaid*, there's a scene at Triton's castle and one of the towers of his castle is clearly shaped like a penis? Or how in *The Lion King*, you see the word *sex* in the sky?[7] Whether you realized it or not, your brain definitely registered those things, but it probably didn't process them.

Similarly, amid all the sponges and soapsuds and boobs, I registered all those things but was incapable of processing them. Remember, I'd already fired a gun the day prior. And now I was on the precipice of becoming a man? My mind was buckling under the weight of all these rites of passage.

When I returned home later that afternoon from my eventful weekend, I took one of those naps that goes so long that it folds into the night and beyond before punctuating the next morning. It was like a self-induced emotional coma meant to help me cope with the sensory overload I'd just experienced. And while this particular sensory overload was a specific kind of unique, that feeling of inundation wasn't something foreign to me.

---

7. There's a counterclaim that it's actually just the letters *SFX*, as in the "special effects" department hiding their calling card in the movie, but if you believe that, I have some real estate in downtown Pride Rock to sell you.

At church and in deeper contemplations about God, I felt just as overwhelmed by the major milestones in my faith. I underwent rites of passage like becoming saved and getting baptized and taking Communion, and while I registered the bare facts of what I was doing, I couldn't process their deeper significance. I wasn't yet emotionally or spiritually equipped to understand the meaning behind them.

After all, what does a baptism mean to a child who rages against the machine of nightly baths? What does eternal salvation mean to someone whose only concept of eternity is the drive from Tennessee to Orlando for a Disney World vacation? And what does Communion mean to a kid who cannot get past his excitement for free crackers and grape juice and then subsequent disappointment when said crackers are incredibly stale? Maybe other kids could understand the importance of these rituals, but I wouldn't for a while, until much further into adolescence.

Being confronted with a milestone moment—whether it's your first collision with pornography or your first collision with the body and blood of Christ—before you have the capacity to comprehend it can leave you emotionally exhausted. I wish these experiences had come accompanied with one of those catharsis naps to mitigate the ideas and feelings that were overloading my growing faith. Because, to be honest, exploring the depths of my Christianity felt a lot like holding that loaded gun: even as I wanted to prove my worthiness, I was still afraid that I'd somehow manage to blow a body part off.

ten

Harry Potter and the Prisoner of McCallie

Of all the details in the Harry Potter universe, do you know the one I appreciate the most? It's not the specificity of the family trees or unspoken rules governing the characters. It's how Harry Potter, the character, required vision correction.[1] For context, I too need glasses; and while I resonate with him on some level about that, the bigger thing is what that tiny detail suggests about Harry the character and the larger story being told around him.

In a world of spells and potions and butterbeer, the glasses remind us that though Harry is the protagonist and prophetic realization of hope for that specific universe, he still has to squint when looking for the Starbucks logo on the billboard like the rest of us. Also, I'm just going to say it: he has very bad taste in frames. What is he even doing trying to pull off the round frames look? Didn't he know that was Daria's corner?

---

1. A close second is how Hermione bypassed a relationship with Viktor Krum and settled on Ron. That's so wildly audacious that I almost find it believable.

What's even more interesting about this is how Harry is surrounded by a collection of people who could make this characteristic quirk go away. Dumbledore, Hagrid, McGonagall, Snape—any one of these people should be able to fix Harry's eyes with no big issue. Even Hermione, the greatest witch of her generation, should have been able to spell-Lasik Harry into 20/20 vision with the flip of a wand.[2]

But no one fixed Harry's vision, and I always loved that. I don't know what J. K. Rowling's reasoning was, but I really respond to the theory that this small thing was intended to be a hurdle that no one would handle for him and, in this, is quietly symbolic of the larger requirement the story was asking of Harry. Because this is an established motif for the story, right? Harry gets a ton of assistance throughout the series, but when it comes to the task of actually dealing with the central story issue or main antagonist, well, that's all up to him, no matter how trying, uncomfortable, or stressful the thing may be.

But as much as I resonated with aspects of Harry, he did spend his middle school years mastering the sport of Quidditch and fighting You Know Who. My middle school experience, conversely, was pretty unremarkable. I had friends, I played sports, but it was still the epicenter of awkwardness for me like it was for everyone else.

I mean, I think we can we all agree that middle school is universally traumatic, right? Sure, the spectrum of trauma might differ wildly, but like death and taxes, an uncomfortable middle school experience comes for everyone. It's like the worst kind of escape

---

2. I'm not trying to belabor this point, but seriously: Ron Weasley over Viktor Krum? In what world is this acceptable suspension of disbelief? It's worse than Jay and Gloria on *Modern Family* or Doug and Carrie on *King of Queens*. If the professors at Hogwarts truly cared about their students, wouldn't they have interceded on Hermione's behalf?

room where instead of a puzzle to solve, the problem is yourself and the puzzle, your own specific brand of awkwardness.

Luckily for me, I was no stranger to trauma given my extensive cataloging of it via popular culture.

The Four Most Traumatic Pop Culture Moments of My Childhood

- The death of Rufio in *Hook*.
- Mufasa dying in *The Lion King*.
- When Sounder crawls under the cabin and dies.
- Learning about the AIDS epidemic through TLC's "Waterfalls."

And though I vividly experienced those traumas, I wasn't that personally invested in the fallout from any of them, so they landed more as body blows and less as shots through the heart. Little did I know that my middle school experience promised to bridge that disparity of trauma.

I attended the local public middle school in our town, and life was decent. I had friends, I played football and baseball, and the school was about seven minutes from my house. Ideal situation. Even the cafeteria was pretty solid—they made those extremely salty french fries and even went as far as having salt shakers on each of the tables, which seemed genuinely insane at the time.[3]

So life was pretty good, and the course seemed set for continued pretty-goodness into the foreseeable future. Certainly for ninth

---

3. Middle school students have as much business dispensing salt from a salt shaker as Ben Affleck does taking marital vows. Both have just an unsparing sense of recklessness.

grade and even beyond. I'd continue along to the local high school where my sister went and where my parents had gone. There was significant comfort in having all this laid out before me, and even more comfort in how I could surf the waves established by my parents and sister, all very congenial people acting as a preface to my similar predisposition of congeniality.

While my sister had attended a private all-girls school forty-five minutes away for her middle school experience, she opted to return to our local public high school. While I knew the very existence of this fact suggested that a change of schools *might* have been in the cards for me, it just didn't seem likely. (If this seems like I'm setting up a gigantic *but,* points to Gryffindor on that assumption.)

Because my sister experienced and ultimately rejected private school, I assumed that I would not be asked to go down the private school path. In pioneer times (totally a thing; just go with it), it would be like letting your oldest child go down the Oregon Trail only to have them die from choleric dysentery. Powers of deduction suggest that something like that might keep a family from sending their next child down the same dysentery-laden trail. But at the beginning of my eighth-grade year, my parents signed me up to take the entrance exam for an all-boys private school called McCallie, potential for choleric dysentery notwithstanding.

Luckily, I had some built-in advantages that would help my chances of not getting in. For starters, there were only a few open slots available and many applicants, so I knew the odds of getting admitted weren't in my favor. For second starters, the entrance exam played a huge factor in admittance. Again, this was definitely in my favor since the test heavily involved math—and *that* wouldn't require any sabotage at all. I *was* the sabotage. Asking me to do math on an important test was like setting out a pan of failure lasagna next to Garfield and asking him not to eat it.

And did I eat the failure lasagna. My math scores were so bad, there was some confusion about what had happened in between the test taker giving me the exam and it being scored by a computer. It was a lot like the feeling after seeing *The Godfather Part III.* In both situations, something definitely happened, and we can all pretty much agree that it wasn't good, but it's unclear *how* the thing happened. There were some theories bandied about in an attempt to explain my scores.

a. I had taken the test, but I was just very, very bad at math.
b. The machine reviewing my scores malfunctioned.
c. Upon beginning the test, I entered a fugue state.
d. I was a savant—not at math, but at flunking math tests, a.k.a. Reverse Rain Man.

At the end of the day, we all resolved to agree with option A and Occam's razor; the simplest explanation was probably the right one, which is that I don't math so good.

At this point, I initiated a confetti celebration of rejection, confident of the fact that I wouldn't be relegated to the social Siberia of an all-boys school where the dress code required button-up shirts, dress pants, and neckties. This might seem trivial, but at the time, this decision truly felt like the difference between a social life and social annihilation.

Not to mention the stakes were pretty high, given that I had just started to understand what I liked about attending school with girls. I wasn't ready to abandon my new appreciation for hallways that smelled like the holy trinity of Bath & Body Works: Plumeria,

Country Apple, and Pearberry. I had even convinced my mom to let me wear Tommy cologne and talked her into buying me some Drakkar Noir.[4] Why would my parents ask me to trade this olfactory bliss for a giant scholastic sausage party smelling of farts, body odor, and feet? Didn't they love me?

Unfortunately for me, though, my celebration was short lived. We received word that I was on the short list for acceptance. It was me and a handful of other eighth graders being considered for three open slots. It turned out that I was so bad at math, I presented more like an unformed glob of clay that could be molded into something better. I was like Brendan Fraser's unfrozen caveman character in *Encino Man,* and McCallie was Sean Astin's and Pauly Shore's characters who just wanted to see if they could turn a primitive mind into something functional. Obviously, my parents were thrilled. To them, me getting in would be like winning a kind of lottery; for me, it would be like the lottery to represent District 12 in *The Hunger Games.*[5]

We were poised to find out my future late in the spring of my eighth-grade year. My parents and I had struck a deal that if I didn't get in, we wouldn't look at another school. This was a zero-sum game. If I got in, I went. If I didn't, I went to school with my friends and all the Bath & Body Works smells I could get my nostrils on. Ironically, I enthusiastically took this deal because again, the math was in my favor.[6]

The results arrived and I prepared to celebrate. I was poised to sprint out our front door, fist pumping like a white guy imitating Tiger Woods, screaming triumphantly into the void of our

---

4. I feel very confident that the fragrantologists who designed Drakkar Noir designed it specifically for a thirteen-year-old to indiscriminately splash all over his body.

5. Except in this scenario, I would not be volunteering as tribute.

6. Or at least I was assuming it was, because I cannot emphasize enough how bad I was at math.

subdivision. I wanted to take the high road with my parents—you know, instead of screaming "In your *faces!*" into their literal faces—but I definitely wanted them to feel that sentiment coming from me.

We gathered in the foyer, and my mom matter-of-factly read the results. "You got in," she said, thrilled but mindful of my devastation.

Instead of running out the front door, I ran into my room. I didn't cry or do anything dramatic.[7] I just sat on my bed and resigned myself to my fate, like a small village in the face of a tsunami. Only in this case, the tsunami was four months away and we were paying for the privilege of it laying waste to me.

I suppose at this point, you might be wondering about my parents' motivation in uprooting my life and asking me go to a different school in a different city with different kids and different educational and social rhythms. And that's a great question to ask. Strangely, it's one I never asked them until many years later.

I think this is because they'd done the work before that decision to earn my trust and faith in them. To be sure, making that decision was a massive withdrawal of that trust and faith, but they'd built up enough deposits over the years to cover it. Throughout the change and even after, I intuitively understood their motivation to be about the educational value of discomfort.

For them, it wasn't a referendum on public schools versus private schools or a fear about my becoming a wayward youth. It was more about recognizing that I had a pretty charmed life, and while that was great, no good thing can come from an existence where you are rarely required to be uncomfortable. And that was me. Had I stayed where I was, I could have coasted off the names they and my

---

7. I mentioned my recollection of this anecdote to my dad, and he said, "You *completely* did something dramatic. You flung yourself on the couch and cried like you were Nancy Kerrigan." So basically the same thing.

sister had made for themselves and I'd have never been pushed to wrestle with any kind of discomfort. This was a privilege I enjoyed, but one I didn't understand the value of. And privilege you don't understand is massively dangerous.

The struggle began immediately. I went out for football my freshman year at this new school with a degree of confidence that at least in athletics, I could maintain some degree of consistency. Sports had been like a faithful golden retriever to me—loyal, reliable, and always chasing away intrusions to my confidence. Even more, sports was the preeminent tool in my toolbox for finding commonality. I had always relied on it as a sort of social cheat code.

This confidence was inspired in part because I'd been told by McCallie students I'd met on tours of the school that I would easily beat out the incumbent quarterback, whom they made out to be as mobile as Jason Street after the events of the pilot episode of *Friday Night Lights*.

In retrospect, I don't know if these kids were evil or if the incumbent quarterback had hit a jackpot of a growth spurt, but the quarterback I met on my first day of practice looked like the Greek God of Option Quarterbacks. To make matters worse, the Greek God of Option Quarterbacks had studied the new playbook all summer and was working closely with the new coach on the intricacies of the triple option, all while I was being emo about my new scholastic situation.

Next thing I knew, I was third on the quarterback depth chart and relegated to the scout team. If you don't know the term *scout team*, these are basically players who serve as crash test dummies for the starters to collide with while getting their reps in and practicing their plays.[8]

---

8. The scout team is like the *Star Trek* redshirts; people not important enough to name, but they provide the function of getting murdered so the circumstances around the principal characters could be artificially heightened.

And as it turned out, this demotion was a precursor for things to come. I spent a good part of my first month at school eating lunch alone and failing to make friends. Not because people were awful to me or the friend circles were exclusive, but because these were muscles I'd never had to flex. I spent a lot of that first year feeling like I was in a weird purgatory of discomfort. I was struggling academically, athletically, and socially, but I didn't have the easy out of centralizing the blame of my circumstances on one thing. My setting may have been new and what it demanded of me unprecedented, but exactly none of it was unfair. So when I self-examined and diagnosed the issue, I found the common denominator at the root of my difficulty adjusting: me. For the first time in my life, my own merit and competency were the only variables influencing my standing. It was in this conclusion that I realized the necessity of finally taking ownership of myself.

In this respect (and in a very generous analogy), I kind of felt like Harry Potter did when he was transported away from the Triwizard Tournament and into the Little Hangleton graveyard. Big V showed up and had Peter Pettigrew sizzle Cedric so hard that he turned him into a vampire and sent him to Oregon to hang out with Kristen Stewart. No one was around to help Harry fight his nemesis: no Hermione or Ron, no Dumbledore, not even Fawkes. No one was there to bail him out, and he alone was responsible for his choices.

I know Harry Potter is about so much, but to me, it's about the process of growing up and the realization that all the layers of protection in your life—your parents, your friends, your mentors, your church—exist to support you, but they do not exist to do your life for you.

The moments in Harry Potter that always move me are the ones that emphasize all the people Harry has around him—in this life and the next. These are beautiful moments because they are often juxtaposed against circumstances of loneliness and isolation. For someone like me, this is intensely comforting, but it can also be misleading. The allure of comfort can sometimes supplant the education that often comes with discomfort.

Leaving behind my identity, my friends, and my introverted comforts felt, at that time, like a kind of trauma. But going to McCallie and realizing that working out my own life meant, you know, actually having to work it out, was the pivot point of my life. If I was bad at math, it was on me to improve that. If I didn't know how to properly put on Drakkar Noir, it was on me to learn the delicate art of strategically applying cologne. Too often, we make the pursuit of comfort out to be noble, and while that pursuit does have value, it's a mirage of a destination. I say that as someone who is routinely guilty of prioritizing the pursuit of things that affirm me over the things that challenge me.

Even now, routine and the status quo feel like freedom to me. Conversely, discomfort and the distress of unfamiliarity feel like ruin. But really, I have it backward. Comfort is bondage; it promises faux relief. Discomfort and unfamiliarity are gifts that provide a type of freedom that buoys, broadens, and always benefits me in the long term.

It's no accident that the summer following that turbulent first year at McCallie, I rededicated my life at a youth camp. If you're unfamiliar, the rededication of your life is when you reaffirm your commitment to God and publicly acknowledge that you will begin striving to be like Christ in a more complete way.

It's like having a gym membership, going through a period of never using it, and then making it a New Year's resolution to start going daily. A lot of times, this leads to a cycle of despair where you set an expectation for yourself that you can't keep, but it wasn't like that for me then. The experience of rededicating my life truly was a rebirth.

As a kid, I repeatedly prayed for salvation out of fear. But this rededication was different. It was a choice made with agency, and it was the last time I prayed to God for salvation from hell.

Thinking back on this now, I realize the power of this moment was in how it dovetailed the spiritual foundation I'd developed as a kid and the realization that I had to put my name on my actions. For the first time, I was able to capably apply what I had learned in church to my actual life within the context of choice. And more, I realized that I couldn't expect anyone to come around and do it for me. Because if a guy like Harry Potter couldn't even get his eyesight fixed, what made me think I didn't need to handle my own problems?

eleven

Knox McCoy, Evangelist to the Stars

If I could travel back in time and talk to fifteen-year-old me, he would be surprised to learn a great many things. For example:

- Chumbawamba was good, but "Tubthumping" was about as good as it would get for them.
- Mark McGwire and Sammy Sosa were *totally* juicing.
- Before long, fifteen-year-old me would start dating that Ashley Weeks girl—you know, the one who'd given him two bloody noses already[1]—and twenty years later, he'd still be with her.

Most notably though, fifteen-year-old Knox would probably be appalled to learn that his writing career was launched not because of his electric prose or a heartbreaking work of staggering genius but from Ashley making him watch *The Bachelor* and *The Bachelorette*.

---

1. One with an open-hand slap to the face and one from throwing a shoe at me. I deserved both.

Like any good husband, I would watch some shows with Ashley that I definitely wouldn't watch on my own. *The Bachelor* franchise was very much in this category, and while watching the show with Ashley, as a coping mechanism, I would write snarky and sarcastic recaps of the show and post them on my blog. Because (a) why else have a blog in the early 2000s and (b) what normal person watches that franchise and doesn't want to write up a snarky recap about it? Mostly my recaps poked fun at the central conceit of finding eternal love over the course of ten episodes, when you get approximately twelve minutes with each other over the course of one week. But TV recaps were still in zygote form, so I grew a modest following of people who also watched the show ironically. So when I think about the show, it's a strange mélange of disdain and affection.

But as someone who has spent a considerable amount of time watching it and discussing it, I can clinically opine that the show itself is less an experiment for love and more a monument to the Big Freaking Sweeping Gesture.

So what does that mean? The Big Freaking Sweeping Gesture is any hugely ambitious thing done to provoke a "Wow!" in the name of love. By virtue, though, this makes it a rotted-out, empty cadaver of a stand-in for love. Episodes and the dates within the episodes are built around the Big Freaking Sweeping Gesture because they kind of have to be. A date built around whether or not one love interest indulges in the forbiddenness of the other's leftovers without securing permission or whether or not one remembers to warm the car up for the other, while very telling, is not good TV.

So why does the show rely on the Big Freaking Sweeping Gesture so much? Very simply, because it is employed as a shorthand for love. They use it because most of the contestants are disillusioned, emotionally stunted people who are truly on the show to get famous enough that they can sell detox[2] tea on their Instagram accounts as social media influencers. But also because there's never an opportunity to develop an actual relationship, much less love.

When you're developing an actual relationship, there are tons of opportunities to showcase love in small ways that make a great impact on what the relationship is becoming. For example, if Ashley and I are in Target and there's someone I don't want to talk to but we're in separate parts of the store, she will text me where they are so I can avoid them. I even have the green light to leave the store if it's dire enough. *That's* love. Or, if I plan on cooking steak and I ask Ashley if she wants me to get steak or chicken for her from the store, she'll always say chicken. Always. But I always get her a steak because I know when the time comes and she smells that sweet, seared beefy goodness, she's gonna want the steak, not the chicken. Where is the love? Here. It is right here in this anecdote.

On the show, though, love is about surprising someone with a helicopter full of puppies all wearing Neil Lane jewelry that you get to keep as you fly to a private concert with Celine Dion, the hologram of Whitney Houston, and Leo DiCaprio and Kate Winslet reenacting their last scene of *Titanic*—except this time Rose doesn't hog the whole piece of wooden debris for herself. She shares, but only because the reality TV couple's love has inspired her to do so. And while this gesture is majestically and extra romantic, it is not rooted in anything real.

The Big Freaking Sweeping Gesture appears in evangelical Christianity too, in the form of "mountaintop experiences," which are basically anything that heightens your faith by provoking a positive emotional response. Revivals, mission trips, youth camps,

---

2. Read: Laxative.

Disciple Now weekends, See You at the Poles—these are all conduits of the mountaintop experience.

And because evangelical Christianity is nothing if not intensely interested in being self-referential, the origin of the phrase *mountaintop experience* comes directly from the Bible: both Moses and Jesus had important transformative experiences on mountaintops. There probably would have been many more, but Bible people wore sandals, and if you've ever worn Tevas on a hike, you know how untenable that footwear can be when trying to ascend a mountain.

The rhythm and beats of many of the most important biblical stories align with this narrative architecture that accentuates emotional peaks. Just look at some of the key events in the Scriptures:

World Creation!
Flood!
Burning Bushes!
Plagues!
Red Sea BUT PARTED!
Water Walking!
Fish and Bread FOR ALL!
Crucifixion!
PSYCH! Resurrection!
Ascension!
END OF THE WORLD STUFF!

It's like the Big Freaking Sweeping Gesture on steroids—only instead of being a charade orchestrated by Ashliiii or a doofus named Troy with a killer haircut and Blue Steel stare, it's an actual covenant authored by God that symbolizes his heart for humanity.

Given this background, it's not a huge surprise that Christians would chase mountaintop moments. And all of that is necessary context with which to talk to you about my own pursuit of a mountaintop experience in the form of converting Katie Holmes to evangelical Christianity.

I always loved Katie Holmes's depiction of Joey Potter in *Dawson's Creek*. That's probably disingenuous. I'm acting like I only appreciated her craft of acting when really, I was also super into Katie Holmes as a teenage boy. But after I compartmentalized that portion of myself, I was also way into her character. She was the girl-next-door archetype writ large, and her hotness was transposed against her best friend Dawson Leery's notness.[3]

Look, the character of Dawson Leery just super sucked. His hair, his face, his personality. All of it was bad. While I love James van der Beek, I vividly hate Dawson Leery, which is complicated because I feel like every character James van der Beek plays is one degree removed from Dawson Leery.

- Jonathan Moxon in *Varsity Blues* is who Dawson would be if he knew how to play sports.
- Elijah Mundo in *CSI: Cyber* is like if Dawson learned computers.

And if you are wondering why that run of examples came to an abrupt halt, it's because James van der Beek's IMDB also comes to an abrupt halt. I could have included another example of how his character on the animated Disney show *Vampirina* is like if Dawson

---

3. In a lot of ways, James van der Beek's Dawson Leery gets a bad rap. And he should. That's the end of that sentence. I acted like I was going to bring some redemptory context to Dawson Leery that would make him seem better than he was, but I deceived you just now, cherished reader. If you are waiting for me to say nice things about the character of Dawson Leery, you will be waiting for infinity.

were doing bad voice-over work, but that's probably an inaccessible reference for most of us. So why are most of the references to James van der Beek's IMDB mostly inaccessible? Because he's got that Dawson Leery stench on him. My ability to like James van der Beek but hate how much Dawson Leery has infected everything he does is a duality that almost feels like proof of God in a certain light.

Anyway, as with Dawson, a wet-blanket central character as the unlikable center of gravity for a story isn't without precedent. Popular culture is replete with examples of them:

1. **Meredith Grey (*Grey's Anatomy*).** If I were Derek, I would have let myself get hit by a car too.
2. **Charlie Brown (*Charlie Brown*).** Lucy and Snoopy are infinitely more captivating. Even Pig Pen is shrouded in a mystery of dirt and stank that's more compelling than Charlie Brown. We should call him Charlie Beige because I'd rather drown in a vat of beige paint than watch stories built around him.
3. **Duke (*G. I. Joe*).** C'mon, he's Community College Captain America.
4. **Bella (*Twilight*).** I've heard cheese tooties with more characterization.
5. **Jon Snow (*Game of Thrones*).** We're supposed to believe the savior of Westeros is the same size as Kristin Chenoweth? Nice try, HBO.

2,942,716. **Ted Mosby (*How I Met Your Mother*).** I dunno, man. I think I'd rather drink leprosy than hang out with a character like Ted. Even within the show, Ted Mosby was the character tax you had to pay to hang out with Barney, Robin, Lily, and Marshall. What a third nipple of a character.

Unfortunately, we're mostly stuck with these title characters, even if the other characters are more fun, because they have to carry the burden of the narrative. They are that pivot point; they are saddled with propelling the narrative forward, while other characters get to provide color and humor to the process.

In a lot of ways, this is why I continuously looked to popular culture for insight and emotion. Church and sports had to carry the burden of holding up my faith and my initial identity, so no room was left for filling out the particulars of my personality.

Which is why I liked Joey Potter so much. While I did love *Dawson's Creek* and did find Dawson Leery to be a hopelessly unentertaining character, Joey felt a bit like hope in a hopeless place. At that point in my life, my days typically consisted of leaving for school by 6:30 a.m. and returning home by 6:30 p.m. to begin hours of homework. The years 1998 to 2001 are a little bit of a pop culture dark age for me, given that 98 percent of my time was taken by sports, church, and school. But I managed to bizarrely hook into a handful of shows, and *Dawson's Creek* just happened to be one of them. I began watching a little bit by accident (because there was no internet or Twitter to remind us about new premiering TV shows), but as soon as I began watching, I was addicted.

So while I certainly liked Joey Potter in the way that boys like attractive girls, and I definitely liked her character as the good to Dawson's bad, I resonated with Joey because I identified with her circumstances.

She was saddled with a life that wasn't great. For her, that meant living with her older sister because her dad was a drug trafficker and her mom had died from cancer. For me, that meant not loving how I had a lot of homework all the time. You don't even know how much homework I had and how much I did not like homework. And the people she was surrounded with were less for her to commune with and more for her to contend with, which is a larger commentary on how introverts perceive the people in their lives. We don't dislike you guys, but man, is it a bummer sometimes when we have to talk to you.

Our situations felt so interchangeable that I was compelled to reach out and start writing Katie Holmes letters. Nothing weird.[4] I didn't cut letters out of magazines or ask for her to send me a piece of her hair. But remember, this is mostly pre-internet, so handwriting a letter was appropriate for the time, like smoking in the 1950s or watching *House of Cards* for Kevin Spacey pre-2017. But in those letters, I communicated the same thing every time, which was that I thought she should very much consider asking Jesus Christ to be the Lord of her life. Remember: I was a good, ambitious evangelical.

I do see now how that was a bizarre approach and, honestly, I should have seen it then. I mean, I don't trust anything presented to me by someone I don't know. I assume every door-to-door solicitor who comes to my house is trying to act out *The Purge* against me. And sadly, I often scrutinize and analyze advice even from people I know and trust by trying to reverse engineer how they might be manipulating me with their advice.

In that sense, I often cringe at how off-putting my letters must have seemed—if they ever even reached her. And how jarring it would be to receive a stranger's unrequested advice about God, religion, and eternity.

But at that time, I'd learned that concerns like those were periphery details. The big swing, the big gesture, the loud effort is the only thing that mattered, and I think this is primarily because it

---

4. My editor is telling me that this is actually very weird, but I swear to you it wasn't.

absolves one of the hard, consistent, quietly thoughtful work of cultivating the realness within a relationship. It's cramming all night for a final exam when you've never actually attended class, because if it works, you get the result you want without the work.

The work. The work of faith is what terrified me. Still does. I'd much rather have the appearance of faith, because I can handle that. But the actual nitty-gritty work of showcasing God's love to someone? That was too real. That required too much. I was never going to get that chance with Katie Holmes, obviously, but Katie Holmes isn't really Katie Holmes for the purposes of this conversation; she's a metaphor. Yes, she's still a real person and remains a real person no matter what Tom Cruise and Scientology want to say, *but* I'm saying that Katie Holmes could have been anyone anywhere else in my life. I'd rather randomly write you letters about what you should do with your life because that's what I was comfortable with. The Comfortable Gospel According to Knox.

It makes me think, with my particular brand of Christianity, was I the Dawson Leery of Christians? The individual whom people had to tolerate to get to the better stuff? Probably. If you think about it, writing dozens of fan letters to Katie Holmes with the noble intent of trying to convert her to Christianity and prevent her from experiencing everlasting hellfire and damnation is a total Dawson Leery move.

My actions weren't without effort; they rarely are. But they were without feeling because it was just a Big Freaking Sweeping Gesture. That isn't necessarily bad, but just like you can't build a love story on Big Freaking Sweeping Gestures, you can't build a faith like that either.

twelve

Knox McCoy, Evangelist to That Kid I Met on a Mission Trip

Interesting fact about me: I'm a *Survivor* fanatic. I've nursed a small pipe dream about being on the show since I was a teenager, but I've never let it bloom into a full-on pipe dream because the idea of actually being on the show is terrifying.

First, I have a fear of spiders, and all the cutscenes of *Survivor* include close-ups of the most monstrous-looking species of spiders. It's like arachnid pornography.

Second, when they aren't showing spiders, they are showing close-ups of exotic snakes.

Third, the sleep sitch on *Survivor* looks very disparate. Lots of shots of contestants lying on uneven bamboo logs while scavenger crabs crawl all around them. You know that dubious stat about how, on average, we all swallow seven spiders in our sleep over the course of our life? I'm convinced that *Survivor* contestants are carrying the statistical load that pushes that number up higher than what it actually is.

More specifically to the game, *Survivor* is where twenty castaway contestants are dropped into remote tropical destinations with little more than the clothes on their backs. They are divided into tribes and they compete in challenges. In each episode, the tribe that loses an immunity challenge event is forced to vote someone off their own tribe. This continues until the tribes merge and it's every contestant for themselves. From there, the castaways are whittled down to two or three, whereupon a jury of the castaways who have been voted out get to cast their vote on who they think deserves a million dollars.

So the show is designed for contestants to constantly deceive one another, but in an elegant, socially acceptable way. So it's not about making it to the end; it's about *how* these contestants make it to the end. That *how* is where the art of the show exists. You can play a great physical game and dominate in challenges, but be a trash pile of a human being socially and you will lose. Conversely, you can be a virtual Mother Teresa, but if you are terrible in the physical challenges, you will lose. Even more interestingly, you can be good socially, physically, and intellectually, but if you are *too* good, people will be threatened by you and you will lose. The precariousness of that *how* in playing the game is what makes *Survivor* the G.O.A.T.[1] of reality TV shows.

The closest I ever got to being on *Survivor* was on the mission trips my youth group took in high school. You're probably assuming that we went to exotic destinations like Honduras or Haiti, but you would be wrong. Taking a youth group overseas is just a straight-up risky idea. Remember 2016-Olympics-era Ryan Lochte? That's pretty much what your average youth group kid is like—a dill-pickled idiot and blank-eyed arbiter of nonsense. You

---

1. I'm told that I might need to explain this acronym, but I'm not going to do that. If you think I'm actually referring to *Survivor* as a hollow-horned animal species mostly native to Asia, then we have a bigger issue at hand.

need to be respectful, vigilant, and aware when traveling abroad, and none of these words exist in any kind of proximity to your average youth group member. So instead, I had the pleasure of traveling to far-off lands like Kentucky (which to be fair, is its own kind of exotic).

As in *Survivor*, there are a ton of unwritten rules for mission trips.

- Don't encroach on another church's turf. That's a very quietly hostile move, like mowing another man's lawn or replying to a text message with just the letter *k*. You want to help out a homeless shelter? Great! You want to help out a homeless shelter that already has a partner church? Uh, what the Philippians?!
- Don't directly interact with other churches in the area unless they've specifically requested it. Treat local churches like wild, sanctified animals, and don't look them in the eye.
- Don't forget to bring the VBS supplies.

Ugh. Vacation Bible School. For Christians, VBS is the Valentine's Day of our calendar—intensely overrated and wildly commercialized. In six million years when the sun burns out and darkness descends on our shell of a planet containing only cockroaches, Keurig cups, and styrofoam, someone somewhere will still be planning a VBS.[2]

I don't want to get linguistic, but even look at the words, guys.

---

2. If I was on a deserted island with a human manifestation of VBS and we had no food, no water, and no reasonable means to attain either, but we did have a gun with two bullets that could secure a merciful death for both of us, I would take that gun and shoot VBS twice. I really would. Once for all the puppet shows I had to endure and twice for all the stale Goldfish I had to eat.

Vacation
Bible
School

A dope word followed by two words that are incredibly discouraging for most kids during the midsummer season. It's almost as if the person who invented VBS felt kids were getting too happy and carefree with their summers, so they wanted to toss in a reminder that *soon* they would be sent back to the hopeless dystopia of elementary school.

I bring up VBS because mission trips and VBS are often intimately intertwined. You go to a place, you help out with some stuff around the community, and then you put on a VBS for their kids, which is a major logistical issue. It's basically telling kids, "Remember that place that visited in the summer and made you go to a school-type thing where you watched bad drama and ate bad food? We're looking for a place like that so we can go every week now!" Not at all great branding.

But beyond the institutional failure of VBS, there are a handful of reasons most people want to attend mission trips:

- To help those with an immediate need.
- To help those with an immediate need but also to try to help solve the larger endemic problem affecting a certain area.
- To paint a wall and/or building, take some awesome photos, and have a dope anecdote to share with others. ("Oh, I've BEEN to the ghettos of San Salvador. I barely escaped with my life.")
- For affluent white ladies to add to their locally inspired jewelry collections.
- To collect souls like a big (spiritual) game hunter.

That last one is why mission trips were like *Survivor* for me; we were there to be immediately helpful, but even more, we were there to be eternally helpful.

The defined terms of our presence were about performing duties and jobs around the church, but the undefined terms of our bigger purpose—one akin to a million-dollar prize—was converting non-Christians to Christians and securing salvations. In the same way all *Survivor* contestants enjoy the experience and playing the game, anyone who goes on a mission trip values the work and experience; but the ultimate goal remains the ultimate goal: to come away with many more notches on my religious belt for the many souls I've converted into the everlasting love of our Lord and Savior Jesus Christ.

Now, mission trips and securing conversions have long been intertwined, but there's a particularly troubling history of white people traveling to places consisting of people of color and ignoring the insidious, systemic issues in favor of prioritizing the more existential question of eternal life. I don't exempt myself from that, but even apart from being a PWP (Privileged White Person), my evangelical upbringing meant that I was always going to see painting walls and holding VBSs as ideal ways of Trojan horsing my way into conversations about salvation.

I still see so many evangelicals playing the conversational shell game of emphasizing the intangible over tangible, practical needs:

"Yes, you need clean water, but what about a clean heart?"

"Yes, you're hungry, but snack on the Word of God, and you'll never go hungry again."

While I don't mean to ridicule the wisdom behind those things, I emphatically want to ridicule people who weaponize clichéd wisdom in this way. It's frustrating to see it, and I can't even imagine how infuriating it must be to hear it.

"Oh yeah, you're right. I hadn't thought about where I was going to spend eternity, primarily because I spend most of my focus on finding clean water for my family. But no, yeah, you're totally right, I should just chill out on the water thing and focus more on the not-hell thing. That makes more immediate sense."

Yet that was exactly the approach I internalized, and it remains pervasive among mission-trip enthusiasts today.

My junior year of high school, a handful of my friends and I were set up to reside at a host home while we were missioning in Kentucky, and that specific host home belonged to one of the church elders. In the lead-up to our trip, we received intel that the elder's oldest son was on a wayward path. I realize that the phrasing of the previous sentence makes it seem like we'd compiled some kind of evangelical dossier on this family—and we totally had. I remember being explicitly told by an adult volunteer that we were expected to leave the house having led this wayward youth to salvation. Anything less would be failure. This deepened our already deep resolve and emboldened our already emboldened mind-sets with the idea that this wasn't just a mission trip; this was the *Saving Private Ryan* of mission trips.

Which, in retrospect, was insane. Putting a fifteen-year-old in charge of anything is a dicey proposition. When I was fifteen, I legitimately thought that *Scream 2* was the greatest cinematic achievement ever. This same person was in charge of escorting someone else to his eternal salvation? To be sure, teenagers are capable of incredible things; but as for me and the teenagers I was running around with, we weren't exactly splitting the atom.

What did I even think salvation meant? While I did recognize the formal definition of *salvation* as a divine gift designed to deliver a person from sin and damnation, salvation wasn't a point on a timeline for me. It *was* the timeline. Everything before someone's salvation and everything after didn't matter because it was the *only* thing that mattered. In thinking back on this, salvation now seems a lot like the infinity stones in the Marvel Universe—certainly the point of all the superhero efforting, fighting, and smoldering, but the journey to those stones might actually be the point.

So we were welcomed into our host home and given the run of the entire basement. We were also given access to the Basement Refrigerator[3] that was stocked with drinks for us.

Over the course of our week in Kentucky, we performed a lot of services, crushed at doing a local VBS, and scheduled many community outreach events. But for me, everything came back to our mission of converting the elder's eldest son (let's call him Avery). But he was proving to be a tough target. I tried a lot of different evangelical techniques with Avery, but most of them were dismissed out of hand:

1. **The *Glengarry Glen Ross*.** This evangelical method emphasizes one's awesomeness so the target will want to be similarly awesome.

   "Look at how awesome we are. Don't you also want to be awesome? Coffee might be for closers but, friend, eternity? Now that is something only for Christians."

2. **The Regina George.** This method focuses on the communal aspect of Christianity and how the target can effortlessly slide into a larger group that will help more fully form their identity.

---

3. I capitalized Basement Refrigerator so you (a) understand that it is important and (b) anticipate that it will be important later in the story. For all intents and purposes this refrigerator can now be assumed to be a sort of Chekhov's Basement Refrigerator.

"On Wednesdays, we wear polo shirts, jeans, and weave belts. Get in, loser. We're going to youth group."

3. **The Willy Loman.** This method is more desperate, and it leverages your urgency in an attempt to influence the target into accepting salvation more for your benefit than theirs.

   "If you don't accept Jesus as your personal Lord and Savior, what will they say about us? We need this, Biff!"

4. **The Filibuster.** This method consists of a deluge of talking and information. Some charming, some admonishing, some hopeful, and some fearmongering. The hope is that the biblical blitzkrieg of information would provoke a decision out of sheer exhaustion and desire to get out of the conversation rather than an authentic desire for redemption.

But all these techniques met with utter failure. Other victories were achieved that week throughout the community and even among other members of the congregation, both young and old, but none of them mattered in the context of my personal mission of getting Avery to accept salvation. As a result, I resorted to the most aggressive technique in my repertoire.

5. **Waterboarding.** Waterboarding is different from the Filibuster for a reason: where the filibustering method aims to passively affect someone into submission, the waterboarding method is a lot more active and concentrated. I could describe this in a lot of ways. I could be delicate, I could be vague, or I could be generous with what happened. But it does me no good to editorialize the fact that Avery got straight-up Christian waterboarded. What's the visual in your head right now? Is it Avery, his face covered by a towel,

sitting in a chair, surrounded by me and my friends while we pour water directly over his mouth and nose? That's pretty much it, except replace "water" with "reasons why he should become a Christian," and you've basically got it.

Ultimately, the waterboarding technique proved most effective because we just wore him down. After a while, for anyone enduring a siege, giving in just becomes the prudent move. We were getting what we wanted, and he was getting the freedom to leave the evangelical hellscape he'd inadvertently wandered into. Classic win-win. But before he was given passage from his own basement, I had to make sure we got what we came for: his soul. Or rather, the audible evidence that his eternal soul would join ours in heaven.

Unfortunately for him, me, and all the other high school boys gathered in that basement, I'd been so focused on getting the *yes* from Avery that I'd short-circuited my ability to lead him in the prayer of salvation. Instead, what stumbled out was the most rambling incoherent prayer of salvation there has ever been or ever will be. It was like Billy Madison discussing the Industrial Revolution. I think at one point, I opened my eyes during my own prayer and saw Avery actively rolling his eyes. That's how buck wild this prayer had gotten. Eventually, I crash-landed the prayer, Avery repeated everything I asked him to repeat to ensure his holy salvation, and he escaped upstairs, literally never to be seen again.

Traumatic praying experience aside, I was proud of myself and my friends for achieving our objective of organically converting Avery in a way that I'm sure Jesus would have wanted (wink). I wanted to celebrate with a delicious carbonated beverage, so I walked over to Chekhov's Basement Refrigerator and opened the door, looking for one of the many cans of soda that had been there all week—not only to find the soda, but also a six-pack of frosty Budweisers staring right back at me.

Suffice it to say that at that moment in my emotional maturity, this was akin to being face-to-face with the Devil. And given the education I'd gotten throughout my life during commercial breaks of NFL games, I knew Budweisers to not just be any alcoholic evil but the King of Alcohol Devils. This was troubling, but even more so because I had to consider the newly converted (wink) Avery. How could he grow up in a home where the King of Alcohol Devils had such easy residency?

I needed to escalate things. I had to think of a way to authentically and incisively speak truth to power in a gesture that was both timeless and provocative. What I was trying to do required a profound simplicity so that Avery's father's heart could be convicted in absentia. I was basically a time-traveling evangelist in this respect.[4]

The gesture I landed on was this: a yellow Post-it Note that simply read, "W.W.J.D.?" With writing, they tell you, less is often more. And in this moment that was also true, but not in the way I wanted it to be.

The events of that night didn't really shape me then, but the further I get away from it, the more impact it has, always affecting me with a wince and flinch.

The road to hell is flanked by a great many things. But most prominently, by Christians talking out of both sides of their mouths. Very unfortunately, I imagine a prominent place for myself there.

---

4. It is a miracle that this hasn't been a premise for a Kirk Cameron movie by now. Someone give me money to write this movie.

The shame I carry when thinking about this story is so malignant that it has provoked me to specifically hate the particular brand of Christianity I was wielding at that point in time. Why? Because I see now that I looked at Avery not as a person, but as an objectified form of opportunity. And in all honesty, my Christianity was mostly built upon this premise: objectifying people into opportunities—both in how they were someone to convert, but even more how they could help buoy my self-satisfaction with my faith exploits. I luxuriated in that self-satisfaction and I passionately sought out opportunities to regale myself in the full splendor of what my faithfulness was.

I framed my holier-than-thouness with a bulletproof context of just wanting the best for those mired in moral squalor, when really, I just wanted to showcase my success at being godly.

I hate myself for having trampled on and broken so many hearts, but I take solace knowing that God can take these legalistic and rude methods and repurpose them into a new perspective that considers and values people much differently. None of that makes what I did right or acceptable, but it does demonstrate the versatility of redemption and grace—even for a holy wretch like me.

The person who should have been undergoing judgment wasn't Avery for not being a Christian, or his dad for enjoying a beer with 5 percent alcohol by volume. It was me. Whenever I read the New Testament now, I'm struck by how pointed Jesus is to the religious authorities and how graceful he is to those outside of the religious hegemony. It makes me reject the notion that imposing your beliefs onto other people is the culmination of love. If it's love, it's a strain of selfish love where you are acting out to make yourself feel safe or brave or appropriate. Influence is something you earn through the work of love, not evidence of it.

I was so ignorant about true faithfulness because I was convinced that it began and ended with salvation. And that fixation completely warped my perspective. I was only motivated by the consequences of disobedience and the eternity of hell, and that was all that was keeping me in line—serving at the altar of fear. Does that really sound like any kind of faith worth having?

Looking back, I honestly couldn't have cared less what happened once I left Avery's basement. I felt like a cool guy walking away from an explosion in a movie—except I wasn't cool and the explosion was hurtful and damaging to everyone involved.

Tying this back to *Survivor*, let me talk about a component of the show I glossed over earlier. As a competitor, you are tasked with protecting your life in the game while engineering everyone else's demise in secret. You have to live in camp together with the very people you are competing against, and if you are fortunate enough to make it to the end, you are held accountable by those very people. Not by the host, Jeff Probst, or a producer or a TV audience; the people you interacted with ultimately get to judge your fate.

In all the evangelical talk about Judgment Day and being held accountable before God, I sometimes wonder if we're all going to be in for a big surprise when it isn't God evaluating the fate we deserve—it's all the people we interacted with along the way.

thirteen

An Argument I Couldn't Refuse

I've mentioned how growing up, I was the consummate good kid. I can count my groundings on one hand, and I never back-talked or waged dramatic, argumentative wars with my parents. But I did have one notable contentious fight with my parents when I was older. It wasn't about politics or religion or generational differences though; it was over the inherent goodness of Michael Corleone.

At the time of the dispute, we were eating at a Sonny's BBQ outside Atlanta. Sonny's was a restaurant chain that was much more prominent before the proliferation of boutique barbeque and designer smokers that let you make your own brisket at home.[1] And might I add, there is no greater proof of conviction in an argument than to find yourself emotionally protesting your point with rib sauce all over your face and hands, too impatient to wait for the hand wipes one gets after the meal. Whether it's about climate

---

1. Actually, that was misleading because I'm convinced it is impossible to smoke a good brisket by yourself. An edible homemade smoker-produced brisket is my white whale, my Chinese democracy. Guy Fieri is more likely to publish a compelling sex tape than I am to make an edible brisket.

change or the motivations of mafioso, a barbecue-splotched argument indicates significantly enthusiastic rhetoric.

I was eighteen and in my first year of college, which means I was swollen with the kind of arrogant naiveté only an eighteen-year-old can demonstrate. That was me. Super mouthy, super self-assured, reasonably well read for a high school graduate but simultaneously unaware of basic universal truths like how diesel gas and regular gas are very different types of fuel.

Ideally, my transition from young adult person to full-fledged adult person would have been an elegant and seamless one, like when Rachael Leigh Cook takes her glasses off in *She's All That* and we, along with Freddie Prinze Jr., realize that she's always been beautiful. Unfortunately, it was more akin to watching a baby horse being born and then trying to figure out how to run. Just lots of stumbling, starts and stops, and eventually, failure.

But this is the process of learning, right? You start and stop. You fumble and fall. You assume and learn what happens when you do that and how it relates to you and me. This is the education of nuance.

This idea of nuance was at the very center of my fight with my parents. The conflict itself revolved around the movie *The Godfather* and its inherent greatness, which wasn't under review. We all agreed that it was a great movie. The disagreement was over how we interpreted it.

At the time, I have to be honest, I felt sorry for my parents. They were debating this movie with me despite an intense intellectual disadvantage, given that:

a. I'd taken a film class earlier that year as a high school senior, so I was basically a critical peer of Roger Ebert.

b. I'd just seen *The Godfather* for the first time.

c. I liked it very much so I watched it again.

Also, you should know that I watched *The Godfather* while I was sky-high on painkillers and dealing with a kidney stone. To be sure, *The Godfather* is a historically dope movie, full stop. But when on painkillers? I could *taste* Carlo Rizzi's betrayal. I could *see* Luca Brasi's social anxiety in different dimensions, and I could *lament* with James Caan's unfortunate back hair exploding out of his tank top, longing for a freedom that could never be realized. So I was uniquely invested in and transfixed by this movie.

Add to this that I had already been fascinated by the idea of organized crime. To understand how I felt when I stumbled upon *The Godfather,* just imagine being supremely interested in the idea of a female doctor living in a post–Civil War frontier town that doesn't really like the idea of a (extremely pioneer voice) woman doing their doctoring, and then BAM—someone hands you a box set of *Dr. Quinn, Medicine Woman* featuring all six seasons and the two TV movies based on that. Suffice it to say, I was heavily invested in the universe of *The Godfather.*

My intrigue with the Mafia was directly connected to the mystery around it, and this intrigue was accelerated by their lawlessness. They were like the Freemasons or Shriners but with more ambition and better style. They were built on initiating disorder and lawlessness, but to achieve this, they had to be extremely ordered and honor bound. To me that was a strangely impressive balance. They managed to occupy a paradoxical space of being elegantly run via inelegant methods. As someone invested in the mind-set that things either were or were not, it wasn't my usual impulse to consider the idea of nuance in making judgments about these characters.

Which is what our argument was about. It was kick-started when we were talking about our favorite characters. I revealed mine to be Al Pacino's Michael Corleone—head of the Corleone crime family that engaged in intimidation, prostitution, and contract violence, and, weirdly, I received some pushback on this selection, most notably in the form of my mom being aghast at my opinion. And I don't blame her. If one of my kids, just before leaving home for college, remarked that they truly admire someone who routinely used murder, mayhem, and the monetization of sex, I would have some follow-up questions to ask like, "Why are you doing this to me?" and "Where did we go wrong with you?"

When pushed, I explained that I admired Michael's resolve and commitment to his lowercase family[2] and uppercase Family.[3] I realize that this is a pretty glib synthesis of *The Godfather* as a movie and Michael as a character, but in my defense, Michael isn't just a cardboard cutout of an evil movie character. As Nick Jonas says, "There's levels." In the movie, Michael is faced with a moral decision and, slowly, he moves down the slippery slope that all antiheroes tend to travel. And it's important to highlight that word *antihero*. Michael wasn't the first antihero I'd come across, but he was the first one that made a significant impact once my consciousness was open to perceiving the kinds of shades of gray that traditionally accompany antiheroes. In this sense, I was imprinted, though darkly, with a fascination for Michael, because Michael represented moral innovation to me.

Now obviously, Michael didn't line up with anything I had learned about in Sunday school or youth group. He drank, oversaw

---

2. The Corleones proper.

3. The Corleone crime family.

gambling enterprises, and murdered people. One of those is a big-time Ten Commandments violation, and the other ones, while not explicit, were violations of Southern Baptist social expectations. But whereas before this point, these qualities would have relegated him to complete villainy, now I wasn't limited to such a simplistic lens. I was aware of a complexity to him that made the question of his goodness much more complicated.

Beyond being an organized crime enthusiast, Michael Corleone was also a war hero who served his country and wanted to make an honest living. He was the son of a mafioso, yes, but he also aspired to a different life. And his father, Vito, even cosigned on Michael's desire for differentiation, but because Vito was attacked and wounded and Sonny was assassinated, Michael was forced to walk back the distance he'd put between himself and the activities of his family. Michael's character was nuanced, and I was beginning to understand that I couldn't just impose my own limited moral perspective onto everything I encountered.

Flipping this around and considering it against a different backdrop, I remember attending a church service where the sermon was about Matthew 8:22. This passage is about a guy who wants to follow Jesus. He yells out to Jesus and tells him that he wants to follow him, but he just needs to bury his dead father first. And Jesus replies, "Follow me, and let the dead bury their own dead."

I gotta be honest: as a Christian, I know I'm not allowed to say I don't like something in the Bible, but I opposite-of-liked this passage. I understood that there was a larger context attached to this verse and that it functioned less as a literal encounter and more as a metaphorical statement about where our minds should be, but at the time, I couldn't get past how it felt calloused.

My family has always been such a huge part of who I am. I'm

a private person, and I trust people very reluctantly. Add to that, I had a great childhood and great parents who vividly demonstrated examples of the kind of person I wanted to be when I grew up. So reading a passage like this made me flinch. Why would God want to do me like that?

But then I realized that not everyone reads this passage the same way. What if I'd had a truly awful dad? Like prodigiously monstrous? What if my dad had split when I was young? What if he tormented me emotionally or physically? Then this verse wouldn't be callous; it would be *liberation*. I'd never even considered that because I'd never had to consider anything beyond my experience. Which is why representation matters. When the only reality we are forced to consider is the same color and belief system as our own, it narrows our lenses and funnels us more deeply into ourselves and more superficially into the reality of everyone else who hasn't experienced the same lives we have.

As the argument with my parents heated up, I became frustrated with them. We clearly saw things very differently. I felt like I was advocating taking a leisurely stroll beyond the familiar worldview and experiences native to us and considering what someone not native to those experiences would do. And I'm sure my parents felt like they were advocating against normalizing someone who liked to deal drugs, sexualize women, and mass murder people. Eventually, in my increasing frustration, I made the definitive misstep of saying something super pretentious to the effect of, "If you guys could just step outside your Judeo-Christian mind-set, you would understand that Michael's not necessarily as evil as you think."

If you are wondering, here's a short list of the things you should never find yourself saying to anyone out loud, ever, even if you are Neil DeGrasse Tyson.

- **"Do you know who I am?"** This is just a mess all the way around. It's a bad rhetorical gambit because it isn't clear if this is a serious question. Also, if you've asked this question of someone, it's set *you* up to fail because the person you are asking either does know and doesn't care *or* they literally don't know, both of which underline your unimportance.
- **"I'm going to get you fired."** This isn't typically used in the right context, such as dealing with a real dirtbag, but instead is leveled at an employee of a fast-food restaurant when you want breakfast but they stopped serving breakfast twelve minutes ago. Pro tip: there is nothing more insane than trying to strong-arm someone at a fast-food restaurant because unless they work at a Chick-fil-A, they are just looking for a reason to consternate you, and if their corporate guidelines support their decision, you might as well be challenging the sun to a staring contest.
- **"Yolo!"** We all recognize this as a grotesque mutation of the once-profound Latin phrase *carpe diem*. Now, it's been co-opted by college kids qualifying their motivation to do tequila shots from a cougar's belly button. In recorded history, there's never been a single instance where someone said "Yolo!" and then participated in an activity that held up against the idea motivating the phrase.
- **"Please advise."** Oh *man*, this is the sassiest and saltiest kind of workspeak there is. It's a very passy-aggressy way of trying to female-dog slap someone through your Gmail. If you regularly use this, I'm not your psychiatrist or anything, but I would recommend working out your issues with the person you are emailing or just stuffing your frustration down way deep inside like the rest of us do versus ever typing out these words.

- **"I'm sorry if you were offended."** No, you aren't. No one has ever been less apologetic about anything than people who say stuff like this.[4] *Apology not accepted.*
- **"Judeo-Christian mind-set."** Maybe it's okay in an academic setting, but even then, "Judeo-Christian mind-set" sounds like you are either about to be pretentious or super boring, or talk about the worst contemporary Christian jam-band in recorded human history.

Let me tell you, there is no one who understands the Judeo-Christian mind-set more richly than a college kid whose work experience is limited to "Sports Camp Instructor" and whose travel experiences were limited to never-outside-of-the-contiguous-US-of-A.[5] I was a college freshman with a GPA hovering around 3.0,[6] not some kind of enlightened philosopher with an acute understanding of perceptions within specific religious frameworks. The word combination *Judeo-Christian* should only be used by people who have passed a test and gained a license to appropriately use it. Otherwise, it's like dressing a dog in a dickey. Sure, it looks like something, but it doesn't mean anything.

For years after this conversation, I was ridiculed by members of my family for my attempt at ascending to the philosophical-religious high ground.

---

4. Note: I say this on the reg.
5. To be fair to me though, Florida is something of a unique cultural experience. Especially PCB. Emphatically PCB.
6. By "3.0" I mean "2.0."

INT. HOME—MIDDAY

House phone rings. Knox answers.

KNOX

Hello?

AUNT JAN

Hey Knox! It's Aunt Jan. How are you?

KNOX

I'm good.

AUNT JAN

How are your mind-sets, Judeo-Christian and otherwise? Still good?

KNOX

I'll get my mom.

So yeah, I definitely lost the argument over Michael Corleone's goodness and certainly experienced my fair share of good-natured familial humiliation. But in the process, I won an appreciation for the complications that can arise when you're trying to articulate what you think.

I am part of a generation of evangelicals who struggle to balance the simplistic spiritual perspective we internalized as children with the more complicated notions and cultural conflicts we experience now as adults. Our gentle souls feel the flood of questions that our minds want to reconcile. But doing so requires a kind of intellectual and spiritual interrogation many of us don't feel capable of.

What's more, many of us feel guilty for even entertaining that kind of consideration; it's another thing entirely to vocalize those thoughts. We wonder, *Is this okay? Am I allowed? Is God disappointed in me for having the audacity to think differently than I did as a child?* But I would argue that God is never threatened when we pursue a deeper truth about him. In fact, he invites us to do it. You could even say it's an offer we can't—and shouldn't—refuse. (Nailed it.)

fourteen

The Heart Attack Provocateur

If someone asked you to name the greatest living actor, there's a good chance Tom Hanks would be nominated as one of the initial selections. Meryl Streep would be in the mix, Leonardo DiCaprio too, and probably Denzel Washington. Regardless of who we land on, I feel confident in saying that if that question were asked to contestants on *Family Feud*, Tom Hanks would be either the first or second answer, and for good reason.

Specifically, I'm fascinated by his career arc and strategy. This is a guy who started out heavily comedic in shows like *Bosom Buddies* or movies like *The Money Pit* and *A League of Their Own*.[1] Then, he pulled off the incredibly difficult feat of moving to more serious roles before going on a monster run from 1993 to 2002. Get a load of the cinematic dominance he unleashed over the course of almost a decade.

Sleepless in Seattle
Philadelphia

---

1. Straight up, the scene from *The Money Pit* when Tom Hanks laughs like a maniac into the ever-expanding hole in the floor is how I respond to stress.

Forrest Gump
Apollo 13
Toy Story
That Thing You Do!
Saving Private Ryan
You've Got Mail
Toy Story 2
The Green Mile
Cast Away
Road to Perdition
Catch Me If You Can

I mean, was this guy serious? Does this historic tear make Tom Hanks a smooth operator or the *smoothest* operator?[2] (I say it's the latter.)

Even after that, he pivoted again to become a sort of white-guy superhero to American dads in movies like *Captain Phillips, Bridge of Spies*, and *Sully*. His characters could pretty much do anything, like a Marvel superhero but at a more leisurely pace and while sporting a dad bod and casual New Balances.

This always stood out to me, because while Tom Hanks was reinventing himself effortlessly, I was experiencing more trouble with the very basic process of becoming an adult.

For example, I made the massive mistake of majoring in English in college. It's not necessarily a regret of the heart, since writing has always been something I loved. And it wasn't so much a tactical error because, for me, graduating college meant playing to my strengths,

---

2. The best, most underrated, quintessential Tom Hanks movie is *The 'Burbs*. Not an opinion. Fact.

and when considering my academic strengths, there weren't a lot of tools in the toolbox.

In this way, I was like Peeta Mellark from *The Hunger Games*. My dude Peeta could bake bread and that was prettttttty much it. Yes, there was that one time he picked up something really heavy and threw it across the room, and everyone watching was like, "Wow, he just took that really heavy thing and flung it across the room." But broadly speaking, Peeta was kind of the turkey burger of ability. Even the thing he was unexpectedly proficient at was artistically rendering himself as a tree or overgrown shrubbery. I don't think Katniss Everdeen gets enough credit for winning the Hunger Games and dragging Peeta's useless carcass around. She's all like, "Peeta, I have to fight off three bloodthirsty rivals," and Peeta is like, "If it helps, I can make my arm look like a dandelion."

And it didn't help anything that the movie cast Josh Hutcherson to play Peeta. While Josh Hutcherson is great, making Peeta good at baking and coloring and having him brought to life on the screen by someone who was five foot five just makes Peeta seem less like an equal to Katniss and more like a really cool Chihuahua that she's developed an affinity for.

My point here is that you make do with what you have. For Peeta, it was coloring, carbs, and carrying heavy things. For me, it was writing essays. I wasn't great at it, but, God so help me, it was my ticket out of college.

When I look back on college, I don't know if there was a person who could have been a worse match for the collegiate ideal than me. I didn't want to be there. I didn't want to lunch in the quad. I didn't want to play Frisbee golf, and I'd rather be dipped in a pool filled with Vin Diesel's sweat than pledge a fraternity.

But this gets back to the point of why I didn't like college: I just wanted to get on with it. I'd attended a scholastically intense high school, and I'd found college to be a similar kind of experience, so I just wanted to proceed to the next portion of life. I'd be lying, though, if I didn't admit that there may have been some other subconscious influences.

For example, growing up as a Christian in the South, I knew that a college campus full of atheist liberal professors is one of the most dangerous places to be. The other dangerous places?

1. A high school party where someone might offer you alcohol
2. In the woods at midnight because of satanic ritual reasons
3. Gay bars
4. A secular music concert

Now, I say that having attended a Christian liberal arts college where only twenty years prior to my attendance, women couldn't wear pants. So I wasn't exactly at Berkeley. But still. Liberal professors be liberaling, you know?

Truly, college just felt like a barrier to adulthood, and I hate waiting out inevitabilities. I wanted to get married and get to work, because I just knew that everything would fall into place from there.[3]

So I did. I married Ashley our junior year of college and did the thing where we attended school while also working and figuring out marriage. For more information on how easy that is, just go to www.terribleplan.com/why_didn't_anyone_stop_us?. If you are reading this and considering getting married while in college, do not do this. There are a ton of emotional reasons why you shouldn't

---

3. Narrator voice: "It would not fall into place from there."

and there are even more financial reasons to not do this, but mainly do not do this because it is super-duper hard.

We were twenty and barely smart enough to live by ourselves without calamity occurring.[4] How did I think I was going to be a competent spouse when I couldn't even confidently light a grill?

Getting married in college is like a movie studio casting their movie with Lindsay Lohan. It *might* work out. Truly, it could. But it *probably* won't. Fortunately for me, it did. I consider Ashley's and my marriage to be the *Mean Girls* of Lindsay Lohan's IMDB. But I know a great many others that turned out to be *Herbie: Fully Loaded*.

In my corner, I had the distinct luxury of knowing exactly what I was going to do after my college graduation, and it had nothing to do with English or writing. My dad and I were going to open a sporting goods store together. It had always been my dad's dream to have one, and we were partnering with a local small-business owner who had worked in sporting goods for years. The plan was for it to be a strategic partnership with all of us bringing different elements to the arrangement. My dad would bring business savvy and financial backing. The local small-business owner would bring experience. I would bring the arrogance and exuberance of youth. It felt like we were all bringing necessary and complementary elements to bear, but, in effect, it was more like all of us bringing different types of flammable materials to the same bonfire.

At the root of the eventual conflict was the fact that I was young, naive, and headstrong while the local small-business owner (let's call him Gary) was older, jaded, and headstrong. I don't know if you guys are doing the math right now, but having two headstrong

---

4. I'm serious. Do you know how many times I almost blew myself up while trying to get a grill lit?

people with overlapping responsibilities is not a great formula. It's like trying to light a firework by shooting a different firework at it. All while standing in a fireworks store.

Gary and I butted heads in a variety of ways over the first year or so of our partnership. He didn't like how I arranged our display showroom, and I didn't like how he smoked in our showroom. He didn't like that I ordered stuff that didn't sell, and I didn't like how he kept reminding me about that. He didn't like that I demanded we have Monday-morning meetings with all the employees, and I didn't like how when we did have those meetings he would click and unclick his pen the entire time.

Also, neither of us was suited for retail. And I can't be eloquent enough about how bad I was at retail. I know there are so many people who have the gift of working in retail and know how to make the experience delightful for both themselves and the customer, but that wasn't me. I'd rather eat a wheelbarrow full of cyanide pills than work retail, because doing it required everything I was incompetent at. For me, it was like being paid to slowly receive the Dementor's Kiss.

So a ballad of discontent slowly played out between Gary and me. It festered and loomed over everything until, one day, I decided that we needed to have a giant confrontation about it. That seemed reasonable. Why? Because, remember, I was reinventing myself first as an adult and second as an English-major-turned-small-business-entrepreneur type. Beyond that, it just seemed like what big-business executive types would probably do in my situation. They'd talk with loud voices, pace wildly, and smack their hands together loudly to physically punctuate definitive statements.

I should probably put this in context by revealing that my dad is a pretty successful and accomplished entrepreneur. My entire conscious life was spent watching my dad build businesses out of nothing and into very successful ventures. In my heart, I always knew his gift didn't genetically follow through to me, but I hoped that in the act of trying to do business things, a dormant competency would reveal itself, proving that when there was just one set of footprints in the sand, it was my business acumen that had been carrying me all along. But sadly, I turned out like a very generic, off-brand version of him—like Mountain Lightning to his Mountain Dew or Jesse Eisenberg to his Michael Cera.

But I hadn't yet given myself over to this realization. All I knew was that I had a degree in English and no writing opportunities. So I was going to play this whole business thing out. I was passionate about our disagreement, and if lit classes had taught me anything, it was that passion usually provoked something. That something might not necessarily be good, but it was indeed something.

And so one morning, I marched into work thirsty for a fight. I walked into Gary's office and started talking with vitriol. And to my momentary exhilaration, so did he. This seemed to affirm that I'd chosen the correct tactic. Maybe I was cut out for this whole business thing, after all! We took turns yelling at each other for a few minutes and, honestly, it was exhilaratingly cathartic. Of course the yelling wasn't solving anything, but there was a visceral immediacy to it that made me feel like things were actually going pretty great.

That is, they were going great until Gary had the heart attack.

After a particularly potent spew of words, I noticed he'd stopped holding serve. He sat down in his office chair and his eyes got big. Like, life-flashing-before-his-eyes big. At first, I wondered if they were large with the realization that he could not handle my truth, but then I realized what was going on.

INT. GARY'S OFFICE—MORNING

KNOX

(Screaming)

You know I'm right!

GARY

(Backs toward his chair, plops down in it. Raises his hand to his chest.)

KNOX

What are you doing? What is this? Are you *conceding*? Have my truth bombs hit their mark, *Gary*?

GARY

(His face is very white at this point and his eyes are big.)

KNOX

Wait. What is happening.

GARY

(Clutches chest)

KNOX

Are you . . . you're not having a heart attack, are you?

GARY

(Nods head emphatically in the affirmative)

I must say, unlocking the "Heart Attack Provocateur" achievement in life makes you really do some soul-searching. And as I searched, I realized that the person I appeared to be was less a person and more a composite of influences and ideas.

At home, I was doing an impression of what I thought a husband was. I would hope it was part Alan Thicke from *Growing Pains*, part Uncle Jesse from *Full House*, and part Jim Walsh from *90210*. But I was probably more Ray Barone from *Everybody Loves Raymond*.

At work, I was doing an impression of what I thought a businessman was. I was aiming for something like my dad, crossed with Simon Cowell from *American Idol*, and spliced with Miranda Bailey from *Grey's Anatomy*, but I was probably more like Michael Scott from *The Office*.[5]

And at church, I was just trying to be the same kind of Christian I'd always been, but just with the complicating factors of adulthood.

To revisit Tom Hanks, I felt very much like his character of Josh Baskin in the 1988 movie *Big*. In the film, Josh is twelve and wants to be older so he can impress an older girl. So he visits an arcade fortune-teller, and hijinks pretty much ensue from there.

The charm of *Big* is Tom Hanks's ability to imbue his performance with two layers. He's an adult man in his twenties but with an essence commandeered by a twelve-year-old boy. It's similar to *Tropic Thunder* where Robert Downey Jr. plays an Australian method actor playing an African American staff sergeant. Hanks and Downey Jr. both execute it incredibly well. But when it doesn't work, it *really* doesn't work. For example, in 2002's *The Hot Chick*,

---

5. Specifically the episode where he burns his foot on the George Foreman grill.

the premise is that Rob Schneider's character, a small-time criminal, and Rachel McAdams's character, a teenage diva, switch bodies
because of an enchanted earring. The premise fails because we're
never convinced that Rob Schneider might actually be Rachel
McAdams; it's obvious he's just doing an impression of a teenage
girl. And even sadder, Rachel McAdams's impression of a criminal
might actually be worse.

I remember during my first year of college being asked what
my social security number was and having no idea. The look on my
face probably supported an answer that would have been "Potato." It
wasn't that I couldn't remember the sequence of numbers; it was that
I wasn't aware of the concept. What was this socially secure number
all about? Was it a four-digit number? Sixteen digits? I was eighteen
years old and had no idea about this number that was essential to
my identity.

Among evangelicals, there's this giant untalked-about void
bridging the end of high school to your midthirties when many of
us try to stretch out the things that were true as kids to the situations
we encounter as young adults and later as actual adults. But that
doesn't really work, because as Ferris Bueller taught us, life evolves
much more rapidly than our ability to keep up with it.

As it was, I felt like a twelve-year-old boy doing an impression
of an adult and trying to say adult things.

"Mortgage!"

"Roth IRA!"

"Aerating the yard!"

"Deacon nominations!"

But I realized that doing the impression of an adult didn't mean
I was actually an adult, and it took provoking a heart attack to arrive
at this realization. Take it from me: there's nothing like almost

murdering someone with your words to make you think, *Golly, is this my best self?*

But truly? My biggest epiphany occurred at Gary's funeral.

Just kidding, you guys, he's totally still alive. He made a full recovery and is in great health. Probably because he left the sporting goods business, and also because he does not have to deal with me anymore.

For the next few years, though, my older sister did sign my parents' birthday cards: "Love, the child who doesn't make people have heart attacks."

Brutal, but fair.

fifteen

The Whiskey and the Bulldog

If you aren't from evangelical waters, you might not realize that in certain regions of the country alcohol and adherence to the Almighty just do not overlap. This is specifically true for me; where I grew up, Christianity and the consumption of alcohol is like oil and water, toothpaste and orange juice, or Taylor Swift and Kanye West. In most places outside the immediate South, alcohol is simply a right, given at a certain age, that comes with responsibility. It's like voting or being able to buy your own cheese or casting Andy Dick in one of your movies. At a certain point, you will have the right to do any of these things, but you must also do them responsibly. Same with alcohol.

This seems pretty cut-and-dry, right? Wrong. Super wrong. Superest of wrongs.

If you'll indulge me, I'd like to do some alcohol-splaining. Around the South and in certain denominations, alcohol isn't a simple concept to understand. In this way, it's like a 3-D element in a 2-D world.

But it comes with some heavier implications. For example, some see alcohol as the Devil's pond water or the sauce of perdition and damnation. To partake of it is to participate in the beginning of your end. Others just see it as an accessory to a low-key good time, like during grill-outs or every time Riggins raised a bottle to "Good friends living large, and Texas forever" on *Friday Night Lights*.

Couple these dueling interpretations with a problematic family history with alcohol, and you've got the perfect ingredients for someone (me) to grow up with no handle on what to make of alcohol. And even a cursory glance toward popular culture didn't clarify anything either.

In movies and TV aimed at teens, alcohol is like one of the Rings of Power from *The Lord of the Rings*. Characters can't have one of those rings and be chill about it. Alcohol is a provocateur. To include it is to contend with it; otherwise you run the risk of normalizing it. To Hollywood's credit, I do see how it's hard to be fair and balanced about alcohol to a youthful demographic. Who wanted to be the executive responsible for making it look like Dylan from *90210* could juggle romantic entanglements with Brenda and Kelly, an inconsistent father figure, *and* an affinity for the finest liquors? Best to take a hard line about alcohol and its destructiveness.

Country music was no help to my understanding either, because the image it created about alcohol was that beer drinking was a subtle prerequisite of masculinity. But being a Baptist, I knew that beer was the Devil in liquid form, so that didn't square, and neither Toby Keith nor Alan Jackson could tell me differently. Even church didn't help. I knew what I was supposed to think and believe as a Baptist, but it differed from denomination to denomination.

- **Baptists.** Alcohol in general was a major no-no. Ginger ale was okay but not if you drank it in a glass and meant it to look like scotch. Root beer was fine, but only poured in a glass because IBC bottles looked too much like beer bottles. Grape juice was fine too, but if left out more than thirty minutes, best to toss it lest you drink any semblance of grape fermentation.

- **Methodists.** Known to (gasp) drink socially. They advocated doing it responsibly, which I'm convinced made them seem more dangerous. It would be like if a Salem witch liked to make s'mores in public.

- **Catholics.** Barely different than heathens. They drank like their life depended on it, and I'd heard from a guy who knew a person whose brother's sister's landlord's repairman knew a guy who did Catholic communion one time and swore up and down that the whole congregation got drunk on the wine meant to symbolize Jesus' blood—and not drunk in the good way. Very much the bad way.

- **Presbyterians.** No intel. Finding out if they drank meant risking having to sit through another conversation about predestination, and if you've ever suffered through one of those, upon leaving it, you'll swear to never do that again. Shoot me into the sun in a rocket coffin before you approach me about predestination.

- **Heathens.** Drank usually the blood of innocents but really anything, anytime, anywhere, and usually during the periods of rest between orgies and their Devil-worshiping sacrifices— which always seemed way ambitious, by the way. I don't think mythical Devil worshipers ever get enough credit for how intense their worshiping is. Baptists can barely be bothered to clap or lift their hands during songs, but Devil worshipers have choreographed rituals and managed to trap and blood-sacrifice animals. I'm not trying to defend Devil worshipers, but can we all at least agree that they seem to work very, very hard?

So again, no clarification. I even took it to the Bible, which only made things more confusing. Like the story about Jesus turning water into wine? This seemed counter to what I was learning about the barbed and evil nature of alcohol. Why would Jesus, the hero of my belief system, be messing with alcohol? It would be like finding out that Clark Kent liked to do a couple of bumps of kryptonite in the bathroom at the *Daily Planet* to cut loose with Jimmy O. after work.

On the journey to understand this, I picked up some generic, off-brand argument that made out like the wine mentioned in the scripture wasn't *really* wine. It was more like very delicious grape juice. I got down with grape Fanta, so I could see how people would get hyped for some grape Fanta at a wedding. However, in my heart, I knew something wasn't squaring up. I'd seen too much and had too much of an awareness about alcohol's effect. Plain and simple, no one would get as excited for unexpected grape Fanta as they would for wine.

So, clearly, my perception of alcohol was on a roller coaster of awareness and acceptance. If I may, allow me to timeline it out to more cleanly demonstrate the ebb and flow of my relationship to it.

- **Ages 0–6:** Unaware. Because I was a kid. Don't be dumb.
- **Ages 6–15:** Aware because of the proliferation of beer commercials during sporting events and inclusion of alcohol in various TV shows and their "Very Special Episode" motifs. And also because it was passively implied through church and afterschool programming to be on the same level as crack cocaine, heroin, and marijuana.[1]

---

1. Which I was only familiar with because of Tom Petty and "Mary Jane's Last Dance." My finding out this song was about marijuana before finding out the truth about Santa tells you everything you need to know about me.

- **Ages 15–21:** Adamantly opposed for two main reasons:
  a. At this point I'd been given appropriate context for alcohol from my parents because it, with a side of infidelity, destroyed both of their homes.
  b. It made me feel extra moral to not drink even though my peers did. "No Heineken for me, thanks. If I want my life ruined, I'll ruin it for GOD thank you very much."[2]
- **Ages 22–30:** Cautiously intrigued. Once I was of legal age, I couldn't help wanting to know what all the buzz (nailed it) was about.

This fascination led me to make my first alcoholic purchase at the age of twenty-one while on my honeymoon. If you are wondering what special libation I purchased to commemorate such a dovetailing of experiences, it was a six-pack of Mike's Hard Lemonade. Are you judging me right now? I would definitely be judging me. The guy selling it to me definitely was.

INT. LIQUOR STORE—NIGHT

Knox puts the Mike's Hard Lemonade on the counter. He has his ID and cash handy. ID to prove his age and cash so there's no paper trail to this purchase.

EMPLOYEE

That's ten dollars.

---

2. A religious teenager who doesn't drink is in the same family tree as an adult vegan or Crossfitter.

                              KNOX

Not much.

                            EMPLOYEE

What?

                              KNOX

Oh sorry, I thought you were going to
say "What are you up to tonight?" and
I was going to say "Not much."

                            EMPLOYEE

Why would I ask you that? We're clearly
about to conduct business, not go on a
first date.

                              KNOX

Right. Totally. *(To self, sotto voce)*
Idiot!

                            EMPLOYEE

Mike's Hard Lemonade, huh? Are you
going to a slumber party for high
school girls?

                              KNOX

(So unbelievably nervous. Like, flop-sweating.)

Right, yes.

EMPLOYEE

(Intrigued)

Wait, seriously?

KNOX

What? No. Sorry. It's not for me. It's for someone else. A female someone else. Definitely not me. I drink different beer. Manly beer, like that (points to decidedly not beer).

EMPLOYEE

That's premixed cocktail flavoring, Party Boy.

KNOX

So can I go? Have we conducted our business already?

EMPLOYEE

Yeah, have a great night, McLovin.

And dear reader, even though I bought it legally and in another town eight hours away from my home, there was still some part of me that expected my pastor, a Baptist SWAT team, and the freaking FBI to kick in the door of our hotel room and arrest/excommunicate me.[3]

---

3. As a postscript, I drank all six Mike's Hard Lemonades that night and vomited. Not from the alcohol, mind you, but because of the incredibly high sugar content. Mike's

So that was my entrée into becoming an active participant in the world of alcohol. Which leads us to another fateful night, nine years later, when I passed through the veil of sobriety and into the realm of drunkenness for the first time ever. It was just after Thanksgiving and my best friend Mark was in town to visit. He brought some nice whiskey as a gift, I picked up some Mexican food, and he, Ashley, and I settled into a delightful evening of catching up.

A classic trope of an inexperienced person who hasn't developed a healthy perspective, right? Think of Jessie Spano with the caffeine pills. Objectively, Jessie was a very smart person on *Saved by the Bell*. But that didn't stop her from making a series of bad decisions culminating with her almost overdosing on caffeine pills, becoming a showgirl[4] in Las Vegas.[5]

There's that old saying often attributed to Mike Tyson that says "Everyone has a plan until they get punched in the face." True for boxing and equally true for alcohol. In terms of my drinking that night, I certainly didn't plan to get drunk. In all honesty, my plan was to not have a plan. At that point in time, I had a lot of work stress.

I worked with a production company that made mini-movies, and we had been through an arduous and painstaking review of a movie about Thanksgiving we were making. It culminated in a three-hour conference call about whether to name a Hispanic

---

Hard Lemonades should test positive for diabetes.

4. In the original draft, I discussed the job of showgirl more clinically, but I was labeled with the word *crass*. WHY ARE WE EDITING HISTORY?

5. Did you know the original idea was for Jessie to be taking meth, not caffeine pills? I always felt like the caffeine pill subplot was a little thin—but holy schnikes, how do you go back to being the valedictorian who fights over what the school song should be and suffers through magic tricks from Max after buying high-grade meth? Bayside just wouldn't have the same breeziness anymore, you know?

character something inherently Hispanic like Carlos *or* something casually American like Hank. You would have thought this was the First Continental Congress with a dash of the Lincoln-Douglas debates because of how passionately this was being argued about.

INT. OFFICE CONFERENCE CALL—LATE AFTERNOON

NARRATOR

It's hour three of the conference call, but emotionally, it feels like hour twelve.

EMPLOYEE 1

Naming him Carlos roots him in his heritage, which is important!

EMPLOYEE 2

But he doesn't have any dialogue! The name is purely for the purposes of the script.

EMPLOYEE 1

Which is why it's even *more* important! The audience should *feel* his "Carlosity"!

NARRATOR

After all the yelling and arguing, the

> script proceeded with the character
> name "Carlos" in it. However, Carlos's
> on-screen appearance was ultimately
> cut for time.

I wanted to use this visit with my friend to cut loose. And I know that sounds like something a burnout character from a movie about high school says.[6] But there is something real and vivid to the idea of wanting to opt out when you're always having to opt in. So I did.

Whatever line I meant to respect with the whiskey, I blew past it. I took off like a rocket destined to explore the great beyond of sobriety and into the bitter abyss of drunkenness.

As a result, my memory of the night has less tangible definition and more caustic associations like headache and the aftertaste of vomit. I do have a vivid memory of starting to laugh too much at something, then running out onto our back porch and projectile vomiting my dinner of Pollo Loco and Maker's Mark into what felt like the next zip code. I remember passing out on the blissfully cold tile of the bathroom, my head wedged between the base of the toilet and the wall, and then later the floor of our living room and kitchen. I don't know in what order, and I suspect it doesn't matter.

What did matter though was the next day. Being the dutiful spouse she was, Ashley had—what's the word to use here?—*accommodated* my sickness and shepherded me into bed. All the evidence of my exploits that night were washed away. Aside from a massive headache, it was as though it had all been a horrific dream.

---

6. I'm imagining myself in this story as Matthew McConaughey from *Dazed and Confused* or Cody from *Step by Step*.

Unfortunately for me, it wasn't a dream. And doubly unfortunate, the duties of the day awaited, which included caring for our neighbor's pair of sexually repressed bulldogs, Darla and Zoey. Caring for these dogs always fell under my purview because, though Darla didn't like me, she did respect me to the point where if she was being obstinate, I could shout her into compliance.

If that sounds complicated, prepare to journey deeper into the weeds of complication when I reveal that the one very most important rule to always observe with Darla was to Never Let Darla See the Back of Your Knee.

Clearly, this raises the question why, right? Why can't Darla, the sexually repressed bulldog next door, see the back of a knee? The answer is that for Darla, the back of human knees presented the most potent aphrodisiac of all time. Knees were the equivalent of the *Sports Illustrated* Swimsuit Edition, anytime Anna Kournikova played tennis, an episode of *Baywatch*, and green M&Ms all rolled into one erotic package. If the back of a knee was seen, she would seize upon it with unmatched ferocity and commence the position and motion universally known as "leg humping."[7]

Anyways, blinded by my hangover headache, I shuffled over to our neighbor's house, found their hidden key, and let Darla and Zoey out into the backyard so they could perform their excretory business. Did I mention it was raining? Yeah, it was a pretty torrential, cold, post-Thanksgiving rain. It was the kind of rain that you confess to love or commit murder in—and as hungover as I was, I would have welcomed the latter on myself. As I waited on the dogs, I sat down on our neighbor's back porch and let the cold rain engulf me.

---

7. If you're still asking yourself, "Why did this do it for Darla?" I don't know, guys. I'm not Cesar Millan or Sigmund Freud.

Nothing was healing my headache pains, but the cold rain had a numbing effect, which I enjoyed. I may have almost gotten pneumonia, but it was worth it for a little relief. I propped my legs up on an outdoor ottoman, looked skyward, and let the rain cascade down upon my face. I wanted to lie in that chair forever. Longer than forever. For infinity times forever, no takebacks. I wanted to vibrate on the same spectrum of my chair in perpetuity and be deposed from this life so I could evolve into a different life form where I could merge my soul with this reclining metal chair and form some kind of superbeing of comforted bliss.

The confluence of rain and comfort with my monstrous headache was so refreshing that I'd yet to notice my fatal miscalculation until it was too late. But Darla noticed. She'd been waiting her whole life to notice.

She attacked my leg with an erotic intensity, and look, I would love to tell you that I valiantly fought her off and protected my leg's chastity with a boldness and ferocity uncommon to our species. But I can't say that. After a few attempts to push Darla from her post, I just let it happen. The rain felt too good, and I knew if I waited long enough, it would be over.

I realize this is a weird story. Essentially, it's about getting obliterated, throwing up Mexican food, having a powerful hangover, and being assaulted by a bulldog, right? And, again, if it wasn't clear, I want to emphasize that you should not do any of these things.

And it may sound strange, but I'm kind of glad it happened. None of the specific elements, necessarily, but the broad effect of the entire experience was quite an education, because (a) it clarified for me two important things about alcohol: that it really could numb my feelings, and that I didn't need to consume it in large amounts, lest terrible things occur. And (b) it showcased to me very loudly how poor my decision had been.

If that sounds like an argument for pursuing destructive ends to better understand the full spectrum of life, it's definitely not. But it does point out how we need to give ourselves space to learn from our mistakes.

Some Christians see grace as a kind of heavenly Febreze that ensures that our souls smell like cotton candy instead of burnt hair, but I find it more helpful to think of grace as permission. Not permission to pursue sin and live in disobedience, but permission to explore the education of our failures without being shamed. Sin is definitely poison, but so is shame; and grace exists as the antidote to those poisons so we can focus on the lessons we need to learn from our screwups. The rigidity and stubbornness that motivates the refusal to acknowledge sin and failure can sometimes be just as damaging as the behavior itself.

While it's true that the legacy of my experience with Maker's Mark and Darla the bulldog is that I need to be careful with alcohol, it's also a lesson about what we become vulnerable to when we make bad decisions. I hope my next mistake—and we all know there will be a next mistake—just doesn't involve amorous animals of any sort. Or vomiting. Pollo Loco coming back up and through the nose is not a delightful experience.

sixteen

The Third Time I Was Punched in the Face

The third time I got punched in the face happened beside my house when I was thirty-one. I'd just sold a T-shirt printing company my dad and I ran together so I could pursue writing full-time—and by full-time I mean a ton of small, odd writing jobs cobbled together to create the salary and time demand of a full-time job. Some of it was work I enjoyed doing, like screenwriting. I love creating characters and articulating them, but fiction feels exhausting. Instead of illustrating the character's mind-set by articulating his smoldering glance and the ruinous craggy rocks of the ocean-kissed cliffs below him, screenwriting lets you just say, "Hank, thirties and kind-faced, is sad."

Parts of this job compendium included less-than-desirable gigs, though, like copywriting. Some copywriting can be okay if you treat it like a challenge. "How do I make this ad copy for a product treating pet incontinence feel like it is ripped directly from the pages of *To Kill a Mockingbird*?" Other gigs have the appeal of a five-alarm fire at an orphanage for disabled puppies. It's just a roll of the dice.

But one component of my workload was truly soul crushing.

This gig paid very well, and it asked me to produce topical blog posts about pop culture. Sounds great, right? In *The Dark Knight*, Heath Ledger's Joker says, "If you're good at something, never do it for free."[1] I'd been blogging about pop culture for years for free—and, in my mind, it was time to get paid.

As you very well know, dear reader, getting paid is good because it gets you the cash monies. But earning any kind of money comes with some strings attached, and this was no different.

1. **First String Attached:** This job had me working directly with celebrity publicists, so the voice on these posts was very carefully considered. I was told to "write as though I was BFFs with the celebrity." Everything about that quote is as quietly discouraging as you can imagine.
2. **Second String Attached:** My writing shift began at 6:00 a.m. and ran until 9:00 a.m. In that time, while imitating the voice of a celeb's bestie for the resty, I had to write eight original blog posts that restated already published news. Creatively ambitious, this was not.
3. **Third String Attached:** Look, I'll just say it—I drew the Kardashian beat. Specifically, the beat about pregnant Kim Kardashian. Thank you for your retroactive condolences about that very difficult time in my life.

I'm fortunate to have very rarely made decisions where I'd screwed up and then was forced to lie in the remnants of that

---

1. Granted, that's in response to him proposing that he should be contracted to murder the Batman, but we're basically talking about the same thing.

screwup. But this was definitely that, and it was comprehensively soul crushing. I felt like Eminem in *8 Mile,* pre-rap battle, but instead of throwing up Mom's spaghetti on my sweater, I had to regurgitate blog posts about the impregnated Kim Kardashian. This assignment was not what I wanted for myself (or anyone, anywhere, really), but I needed those aforementioned cash monies.

At the beginning, I dutifully worked the job because it was a job and my parents taught me to do my best at everything. I even considered Bible verses I'd memorized as a kid like Colossians 3:23: "Whatever you do, work at it with all your heart, as working for the Lord, not for human masters." I felt pretty sure that whoever authored Colossians wasn't talking about doing your best work as the beat reporter for a pregnant starlet who rose to prominence because of an explicit sex tape she made with Brandy's brother, but I *did* feel like it was applicable to this situation because, as I was taught, the Word of God never returns void.

After a few weeks, my Scripture-infused resolve weakened. I stopped taking the gig seriously because every time I submitted a post for publication, it was like a tiny piece of my soul was committing ritual seppuku with a dull butter knife.

Sometimes, I'd show up online late for a shift; other times, I'd only submit four or five posts instead of the requisite eight. At least once, I just didn't even show up for my shift at all.

So I shouldn't have been surprised when I got a phone call late one afternoon from my editor.

EXT. SIDE OF MY HOUSE—AFTERNOON

Knox answers his phone. It's a phone call from his editor, Carol.

KNOX

Hey Carol.

CAROL

Hey Knox. Do you have a moment to chat?

KNOX

Definitely. How are you?

CAROL

So we're going to be letting you go.

KNOX

Go where? Like on a trip?

CAROL

Kind of, I guess? Like on a trip away from the job we pay you for except that you can't come back.

KNOX

You're firing me?

CAROL

As it turns out, you haven't really been doing what we've asked, and we kind of need freelancers to do exactly what we ask.

KNOX

Wow. Okay. Well, it's probably for the
best.

CAROL

It certainly is for us.

KNOX

Settle down, Carol.

(The line goes dead.)

KNOX

Hello?

I know this isn't an actual, physical punching of the face like the others. But when the only job you've ever been fired from is a sixth-rate internet gossip blog, I gotta say, it stings the pride infinitely more than a fist to the nose.

And honestly, this is more what I fear now that I'm older. Instead of visceral and physical pain, I fear the conceptual and existential. I don't fear someone punching me in the nose or ear; I fear failure and rejection. I can't help wondering if those endure because, while we can hedge against physical threats, the immaterial ones tend to be the most haunting.

And why is that? Is it because at a certain midlife-ish age, you aren't pushing for exploration or subversion; you really just want balance? With this job, I was forced to balance good with bad. I desired freedom, but one that needed to be subsidized with a debilitatingly embarrassing writing gig. My failure was, I wasn't wise enough to reconcile my discomfort with the paycheck, and I wasn't mentally tough enough to reconcile the choice I made with my immediate reality. So I just stagnated in the job until a choice was made for me. But I never realized that submitting to the stagnation was making a choice.

Dear reader, I hope you are never forced to deal with being fired from a terrible writing job. It won't be the worst thing that ever happened to you, but it is a destabilizing event. "If I'm not even good enough to write about pregnant Kim Kardashian, am I qualified to write about anything?"

So it might seem silly when I say that it waged psychological warfare on me. But it did so because the complacency that I'd given myself over to professionally paralleled a similar kind of complacency I was experiencing in my faith.

I still believed in everything that typically composed a generic version of an evangelical's faith, but I did it with the passion of someone signing the paperwork at a house closing. I wanted the house, but were all these signatures really necessary?

Also, my faith was crammed into a crowded space. Kids, work, getting fired—that stuff takes time, you guys. But secretly also? I was complacent because I was bored and dissatisfied with the faith I'd made for myself.

Eventually, we all have to decide if the things we believe work within the larger patchwork of our lives, right? My dad calls it *situational ethics.* You believe stealing is wrong, but if you could steal and no one would be hurt and no one would find out, would you do it? If you would steal, then you probably never really believed in the wrongness of it in the first place, just the shame that would come with potentially getting caught.

In the same way, I agreed with the notion that my faith was important, but actually practicing and prioritizing it? I was less enthused about that.

You know the difference between discovering a new TV show to binge versus watching *The Office* for the eleventeen trillionth time? That's what my faith felt like. There's wasn't any enthusiasm for it, just like I don't think anyone sets out to build their night around watching Jim and Pam's wedding episode on a loop. You kind of just end up there because it's easy and familiar. But as comforting as easy and familiar can be, you start to feel the discomfort that asks, "Is this it?"

My homogenized and commercialized Christian experience just wasn't enough anymore, and I bristled against a discomfort I couldn't put my finger on. And if this reads like a criticism of evangelicalism or commercial Christianity, it's not meant to. I've definitely got criticism to levy, but that lack of enoughness? That was my own doing.

To be sure, there were issues and doubts and questions I just didn't do anything with. I didn't challenge or investigate. I just met those feelings with an "Oh well, it's probably not that big of a deal." Maybe they weren't individually. But when compressed together, this rat king of discontent was a big deal for me.

Was creation literal?

Should women really not be in ministry?

Why was everyone so chill about Solomon seeming like such a horndog?

Is hell real?

If the Bible is authoritative, why does it contain contradictions?

I wasn't necessarily disagreeing with any of these things; I just wanted to ask the question, but I'd been conditioned to feel like that was an incorrect and disobedient impulse. Because to ask meant to doubt and to doubt made you like that Thomas fella who always seemed characterized as the next-sketchiest disciple after Judas, even though now, with the benefit of age, Thomas is the disciple I most identify with. Not because he doubted, but because he thought it was a worthy thing to articulate a doubt *so that he could better understand.*

My discontent and doubts, they weren't the work of the Devil or scarlet letters I'd have to brand myself with. Rather, they were breadcrumbs leading me to a faith that required more work, but they would also lead me to a faith that was infinitely more realized and abundant than I ever could have thought.

If you look at the origins of any revolution throughout history, they all come complete with a preexisting context of discontent, and I think that was true for me as well. Professionally, getting fired was a result of my discontent with the work, but also of my own complacency. This sparked a revolution within me about who I was going to be and what I was going to be involved with.

And this was the beginning of an evolution in my faith. It was no longer the ideological monolith I'd passively orbited my whole life. I knew it wasn't in me to write in the voice of a celebrity's BFF; and even more, I couldn't live out my belief in the voice and manner of someone not consistent with who I was. That's not a criticism of those who ask fewer questions; rather, it's an acknowledgment that if God really did knit me together complete with my inquisitive and wondering nature, did he really want me to deny that design feature?

As with my early collection of jobs, when I dove deeper into what all that wondering and questioning provoked, I saw an elaborate mosaic of tiny ideas, experiences, and beliefs that worked together to create a beautifully profound picture that I'd never allowed myself to see. Each of these things themselves wasn't enough to sustain the entirety of a faith, but together they were beginning to form something really quite lovely.

seventeen

The Sidekick Corollary

I'm a professional podcaster. Does that sentence feel as strange to read as it does for me to type? It sounds like one of those incredibly dubious jobs you'd see on *The Bachelor* or *The Bachelorette*. Like when a guy introduces himself as an "entrepreneur" but he clearly spends more time on his hair and body than I've ever spent on anything in my life.[1]

If you aren't familiar with me or what the word *podcast* means, let me explain. My show, *The Popcast with Knox and Jamie*, has been running on Wednesdays since 2013; and on it, my partner, Jamie Golden, and I talk about popular culture. TV, movies, books, music, celebrities . . . all the things. Primarily we try to talk about stupid things in an intelligent way, but really, this is just an elaborate con for both of us to justify our interest in pop-cultural elements.

We started with very few listeners, but we've been fortunate

---

1. I have a side theory related to *Shark Tank*, that the more pale and disheveled you are, the more likely you are to get a deal with a Shark because clearly you spend most of your time in the company of spreadsheets. As a culture, we've evolved to associate spreadsheet familiarity with business acumen. I just don't trust a tan, shredded, California nine named Brad Chadley and his similarly attractive business partner, Chad Bradley, to run a successful company, and you can't make me.

enough to collect a substantial listener base who resonate with our mission statement of "educating people on things that entertain but don't matter." So much so that we've been able to quit our day jobs to fully devote ourselves to the show. Which is great, because what could be better than being able to monetize the thing you are most interested in? Granted, some self-consciousness comes with trying to deftly describe what I do for a living. There's nothing like trying to explain to someone over the age of fifty not just what a podcast is, but how it is you make money from it. Just trust me, Aunt Charlene, our bills are getting paid, I promise.

This professional evolution has resulted in me having to reconsider how I consume popular culture. After all, I can't just watch, read, or listen to things; I also have an obligation to listen with an observational and curational ear. I am a purveyor of pop culture. Like a sort of Stone Phillips or Tom Brokaw for your ears. That's right, I'm pretty much trying to talk to you about how hard I work at watching movies and TV and reading books.[2] This new directive, combined with years of already compiled knowledge about popular culture, led me to view it in a different dimension. My new motivations and perspectives let me see beyond the superficiality of shows like *Who's the Boss?* and *Charles in Charge* and into the essence of what motivated the story and the characters, and specifically what the eighties seemed to be saying about the viability of young-to-middle-aged men as caretakers and homemakers.[3] This newfound

---

2. I'm basically a modern coal miner but of movies and reality TV. Same danger level basically.

3. Actually, these shows aren't saying anything substantial about the dynamics of gender roles in the home as much as they are a probable reaction to the success and influence of Michael Keaton's 1983 movie *Mr. Mom*, a movie I watched more than 289 times. "*Your mom calls the vacuum cleaner Jaws?*"

prism of consideration helped me recognize recurring quirks and tropes, most notably in sitcoms, but definitely throughout culture.

So let's think about this broadly. All the sitcoms I watched as a kid had pretty accessible contexts:

- White people doing white people things.
- Black people doing mostly white people things. (Excepting *A Different World*, which I still love to this day because you can tell they knew what kind of a hill they had to climb simply by the name of the show. It's like they knew that the average white TV viewer would be grouchy about a black family that wasn't the Cosbys, so they literally named the show in a way that told white people, "This is going to be a different context than you are used to.")

All the shows leveraged familiarity. There were familiar beats and familiar rhythms and familiar character archetypes, all combining to form a warm bubble of familiarity. The story beats, the pacing of the shows, the laugh tracks—all were similar.

But the primary way all these sitcoms hooked you was with familiar character archetypes. Because you're way more likely to commit to watching a show if you can identify with one of the principal elements. So let's examine some of these principal elements.

- **The Central Character.** This one is easy, right? It's the main character upon whom most of the storylines hinged. On some kids' shows, we see dual central characters: one for adults to identify with (think Danny Tanner) and one for kids to identify with (think DJ Tanner).

Others, like *Perfect Strangers,* were two-handers in the sense that Larry and Cousin Balki were both central characters; but because they represented different hemispheres of the brain, they essentially functioned like one supersized central character.

- **The Supporting Central Character.** These characters are essential to the plot and context, but only in connection to the central character. Their subplots usually exist to fill the B and C plots of episodes, but they have importance only in the way they relate to the central character. (Think Shawn Hunter from *Boy Meets World.*)
- **The Useless/Redundant Kid.** Since all these sitcoms catered to kids, the casts were flush with kids so viewers like me could find some kind of foothold with one of them. And since acting, writing, and kid involvement is such an inexact science, they just threw a ton of kid actors at the wall to see what stuck. (Think Judy Winslow from *Family Matters.*)
- **The Sidekick.** This is where things got interesting for me. You have these layers of normalcy and familiarity: normal contexts, normal settings, normal characters framed by normal supporting characters. It's a lot of situational normal. Which is where the sidekick character comes in. They put the *com* in the sitcom, so they exist to be hyper-weirdo savants who are plot hijinks made manifest. (Think Steve Urkel.[4])

---

4. Steve Urkel is the most fully formed realization of this character, but he's almost too fully formed in that the show almost lost the thread of the base story in order to build more things around Steve's hyper-popularity. There's a great *Key & Peele* sketch about this dynamic, but I'm not recommending it here because it has some NSFKM (not safe for Knox's mom) language.

As I looked back on the shows that defined my youth, I began to see that these zany/goofy/quirky sidekick friends always came concomitant with a fully realized, relatably normal central character. And it dawned on me how genius this was.

See, the sidekick's function was two pronged: (a) to reinforce the main character's normalcy, and (b) to propel storylines and plots into interesting directions, test the main character's resolve, and provide a context for poignant resolutions to be had.

I was almost disturbed by how perfectly compatible the whole arrangement was. The main character gave me a baseline of behavior, which then allowed for the sidekick's behavior to be that much more influential, while the sidekick contextualized and heightened the main character without eroding their relatability or likability.

Think about *Finding Nemo*. Could you have lasted an entire movie with Albert Brooks as a clownfish screaming about his son? Me neither. Personally, if I were Nemo, being in an aquarium at a dentist's office might be preferable to hanging out with Marlin for the rest of my life, but that's me. My point is, Dory contoured the most irritating parts of Marlin and helped tease out what was great about him as well as provoking a lot of the most heartfelt moments of the movie. For this, she is an all-time sidekick character.[5]

So let's think a little more about these sidekick characters. We get very little in the way of biographical details, but I saw them enough to understand some basic parameters.

---

5. Now, did this mean there should have been a Nemo sequel about her? No. No it does not.

1. Sidekicks are usually socially undesirable.

Again, this undesirableness establishes the main character's coolness both (a) in the way they charitably allow someone like the sidekick to hang around them and (b) in how the sidekick's presence reinforces that the main character is the alpha of the show and is relatably normal.

Donkey from *Shrek* is a great example of this. While Shrek is an ogre, he exists as an ogre within a world where other communities of ogres also exist. So he fits as a traditional protagonist. Conversely, Donkey is a standalone peculiarity. He's loud, obnoxious, and most notably, strange. All these things work together to heighten the idea that Donkey is a social disaster, as well as increase our desire to root for Shrek despite his ogreness.

2. Sidekicks have strange names.

Cory Matthews had Minkus on *Boy Meets World*. Will Smith on *The Fresh Prince of Bel-Air* had DJ Jazzy Jeff, and Zack Morris on *Saved by the Bell* had Screech Powers. These names suggest a deeper, perhaps ultimately unknowable strangeness hidden within each character.

As a principle, this may seem like a cheap gimmick, but even in real life names very much feel like harbingers of someone's place on the social spectrum. Think of NFL quarterbacks:

- Tom Brady
- Cam Newton
- Peyton Manning

- Randall Cunningham
- Joe Montana

Even if you don't know football, these names sound straight-up awesome, so the fact that the people they belong to are also awesome feels correct. Separate these names from whom you associate them with. If an email shows up in your inbox with one of these names on it, isn't it pretty much a sure thing that you're opening it? Completely definitely.

Now, hear these names:

- Blaine Gabbert
- Blake Bortles
- Chris Weinke

If I get an email for any of these people, I'm assuming it's

a. to ask me for money;
b. to join their direct-sales company that sells vape pens exclusively on Facebook;
c. ending up in my spam folder because it mentions things like "sexual performance."

But beyond being just strange, sidekick names subconsciously reinforce the character's permanent status on the fringes of the social spectrum.

Because of their names, our instinct tells us that Harley Quinn, Andy "The Nard Dog" Bernard, and Dwight Schrute have all experienced the social marginalization inherent to the sidekick character.

3. The arrival or presence of a sidekick usually portends hijinks or shenanigans.

Trace enough plot points back to their origins, and you'll find that the sidekick has a fair amount of involvement in their inception. In fact, we get the feeling that if the main character could ever shed the burden of these bizarre friends, their life would become much more serene and normal. Naturally, this notion never occurs to them, so they don't.

Think of Jerry Seinfeld. How many bowls of cereal were interrupted by Cosmo Kramer? The door swings open and Kramer slides in with a bizarre urgency that usually sets the events of the episode into motion. But that entrance is apropos of the larger point here: sidekicks have a way of bursting into the lives of the main characters and initiating complication.

4. Sidekicks are incredibly self-satisfied and largely unaware that they are socially marginalized.

When you think of the best sidekick characters, you'll notice they possess an incredible confidence that is only exceeded by their ignorance to the fact that they are functional weirdos. To them, the world is in the wrong and they are in the right; and while they might be technically correct, the fact is overwhelmed by their larger disconnectedness. And even more, you get the sense that the sidekick thinks they are actually the star of their own story.

Take Dwight Schrute from *The Office*. Beets and beet farms and whatever else he and Mose do on their beet farm might be great, but their presentation is off-putting. Even more, Dwight seems to be very clearly convinced that all his Dunder Mifflin coworkers are just details in a story oriented around him.

So as I reflected back more and more on these influential shows and began to consider them through a scrutinizing lens that only a true podcasting professional could wield, I saw how ubiquitous this sidekick character archetype was. And even more, I realized that it had a much closer proximity to me than I had ever realized.

Even though the sidekick character is a creature of fictional universes, it feels very much a part of modern culture, specifically in modern evangelical culture.

Just look at the relationship between popular culture and modern evangelical Christianity. In my life, both of these were characters in my story, but I hadn't really cast them into any archetype. They both existed independent of each other. But really, that relationship has always felt fraught, given that the culture of modern evangelicals is defined by its separate and inverse relationship to popular culture. Even as a kid, this was an obvious subtext to pick up on.

For an evangelical like me, there were regular movies and then Christian movies. The "Christian" label was less a genre signifier than a code for knowing that the movie itself was going to be 45 percent worse across the board than your average secular movie. Not because of its Christianness, but because the people behind the movie treated the preexisting Christian context as something so noble that it exempted them from attempting a compelling story. As though its mere existence was an accomplishment, excusing their less-than-stellar effort.

Often with Christian entertainment, the goal is for something to be affirmational more than it is to be authentic or artistic. Said out loud, most would agree that this is a terrible principle to abide by, but it persists to this day because of its simplicity.

Christians at odds with popular culture can find a significant amount of spiritual fulfillment in the rejection of anything even obliquely related to popular culture. It's a pass-fail proposition for many evangelicals, and if the first descriptor of a book, movie, album, or TV show isn't "Christian," the referendum against it is already set.

That's the very issue with Tim Tebow. Tim Tebow was a fine college quarterback. He was tough, gritty, and inspirational— the definition of a leader. But homeboy can't throw a fifteen yard out. This is because his throwing motion is like Uncle Rico's from *Napoleon Dynamite*. And that's okay! Being a professional NFL quarterback is hard. There are only thirty-two of those jobs, so it's kind of the upper echelon of performance.

But for some evangelicals, we can't reconcile the reality of Tim's athletic ability with the greatness of Tim as a person. Tim Tebow is as idealized a Christian athlete as there has been in my lifetime. He genuinely seems like someone with a heart for people and a passion for repurposing his fame for genuinely good things, which is amazing. But this can shade certain perceptions of his quarterbacking skills in a way that isn't rooted in any kind of reality. For the NFL, it's pretty simple; he is the author of more wounded ducks than the most accomplished duck hunter, but for Christians, there is no chill to be had here.

And as much as I've always been aware of this division of pop culture and church, I never realized how I'd misinterpreted things. To me, growing up, evangelical Christians were always the normal Danny Tanner–like protagonist. We were the pulse of American society and always ready to sit down for a heart-to-heart with others when necessary. After all, we carried the mantle of morality and values. A heritage of exceptionalism furthered this idea. We were the central players pushing things forward, and popular culture was just this zany supporting character who sometimes intersected with us for a little excitement. But it never dawned on me that I had this wrong. We weren't Danny; we were the Kimmy Gibblers. And the more I considered this, the clearer it became.

Were we socially undesirable?

There's a reason the judgmental, overbearing, out-of-touch Christian is a cliché. That isn't a fair representation of everyone under the evangelical banner, but this type of Christian has run amok enough that the rest of us have to overcome it. Sadly, the application of the "Christian" tag doesn't necessarily mean you're dealing with someone to be trusted. For a great many people who don't identify as or know evangelicals, sometimes the label of "Christian" is a lot like the label "butthead."

Did we have strange names?

This one was more opaque, but yeah, sometimes! It can be as simple as naming your child Hezekiah Bramblewood the Baptist or Matthew MarkLukeJohn Smith.

But also, at my church, everyone was called Brother and Sister, which is confusing to a kid, and also to people not familiar with church vocabulary.

Even in a different sense, calling ourselves "the saved" or "the chosen" or "the elect" can be a bit different for the uninitiated. That's definitely not as obvious as being named Barney Fife or Shaggy Rogers, but Christians tend to speak with names and labels that can further enhance disconnectedness.

Did our arrival on the scene usually mean hijinks would ensue?

Yeah, a little bit!

Let's be honest, guys: we Christians have a way of co-opting everything into a commentary on your faithfulness or lack thereof.

Even the most basic thing, like fashion, isn't immune to this. If you're an evangelical Christian, why shouldn't what you're wearing also fulfill a secondary purpose of telling people where you land on the faith scale? This impulse led to a deluge of truly regrettable T-shirts that leveraged brand familiarity and twisted it into something vaguely Christian.

- Instead of a shirt with the Starbucks brand logo, it was the word *Sacrificed.*
- Instead of a shirt with the Tide brand logo, it was the word *Tithe.*
- Instead of a shirt with the Facebook brand logo, it was "Faithbook: Add Jesus as Your Friend"
- Instead of a shirt with the Reese's brand logo, it was *Jesus* in that same font.

I don't really know what the evangelical endgame is for shirts like this. If the intent is to emphasize how everything has less than six degrees of separation between it and Christianity, that's fine, I guess. But it feels like a tenuous faith-based connection. Taking something that is secular and making it look Christian is a specific kind of tomfoolery where Christians think we can just graft ourselves onto something and it will totally be fine. But when we do this, we fail to remember that the God we serve is a creator, not an imitator, so why is Christian culture content to consistently reappropriate the runoff of popular culture in a less interesting way? If it's an effort to honor, it's a misguided attempt that doesn't honor God as much as it honors the navel-gazing impulse of Christians to be Christian.

It's why Halloween can't just be Halloween. Churches have to put their spin on it. Because even Halloween, as rooted in pagan tradition as it is, is an immovable force. Even churches know not to mess with people and their license to eat candy. At some point, churches knew they had to embrace this tradition but they wanted to do so with a twist. So they invented Halloween-adjacent holidays that coincide with the more general holiday: Harvest Festival, Holy Ghost Weenie Roasts, Hobo Suppers, Hallelujah Boo-yahs, and Trunk or Treats.[6]

These are all fine events. But they are complicated by the Christian necessity to recodify something as inappropriate because it exists beyond the realm of the church. And while I understand why they do it, behavior like this has only served to highlight the bizarre funhouse-mirror prism the general culture tends to see us through.

---

6. Sadly all of these are real names, which means there is at least one church out there that thought "Halloween" was too much, *but* that coordinating and marketing an event called a "Hobo Supper" was perfecto.

And this lack of perspective relates neatly with the last principle of sidekick characters.

Are Christians full of self-satisfaction and unaware of their marginalization?

Yeah, check mark on that too.

As a Christian, I can testify to the immense pride we've taken in our cultural marginalization, but that pride comes from a misunderstanding of how we've interpreted the word. We have been marginalized not because we're being persecuted but because of the broken method we use to try to connect with the world and the culture surrounding us.

We tell ourselves our beliefs are persecuted despite being over-represented in government, and this is especially tone-deaf when compared to the actual persecution and marginalization of people of color, women, and immigrants.

Why? Because the narrative of our own persecution and marginalization absolves us from cleaning up our own house and course-correcting our own missteps. Isn't it just easier to tell ourselves that because non-Christians are heathens and enjoy the comfortable confines of their myriad sins, we can't see eye to eye? But really, we prefer the one-sidedness, because it insulates us and liberates us to be less a central character and more like a weirdo neighbor kid with a penchant for cheese and barging into your living room unannounced.

I think there's a tendency to hear the notion that Christians are just sidekicks and take that as sacrilege or insult. It's a natural impulse to want to be the star, the lead protagonist the story is built around, and even more so when the story contains holy and eternal implications.

But really, weren't we always meant to be sidekicky? As believers in a faith that espouses attaching ourselves to God and the principles of his Son, Jesus, and even playing the role of sidekick to our own selfish nature, to me it seems Christians have always been destined to come alongside in a supporting role to enhance and improve things for others. It is my genuine hope to influence and improve everyone around me in a way that heightens the best parts of them and their story and teases out the goodness inherent to all of us. Personally, I love the idea of playing the role of Samwise Gamgee to modern culture's Frodo Baggins. Strong both in heart and spirit, steadfast in love, and able to resist the pull of evil? That's the kind of noble character I'd be honored to share a description with.

eighteen

The Cancer

When I was twenty-seven, I came to the conclusion that dinosaurs couldn't have been in the Bible. I know some people still believe they were and they were drowned in the Flood, and that's a fine and per-fectly acceptable answer for them. It wasn't for me, but I won't deign to speak about how all walks of life factor into the Great Timeline. You can believe there were yetis in the Bible for all I care.[1]

I'm just saying that in constructing my specific faith, I came to a crossroads where I had to reconcile how the people in the Bible intersected with the principal antagonistic elements from *Jurassic Park*. And when I did that considering, it was my conclusion that they didn't exist on the same timeline. For me, a lot of it came down to how none of the stories in the Bible mention dinosaurs. I know behemoths and leviathans are talked about in a very offhanded way, but I just can't believe that those stray comments were meant to encompass the existence of all the dinosaur species supposedly

---

1. I do have to be honest though: yetis in the Old Testament would certainly be a boost. Can you imagine if your perception of the David and Goliath story wasn't just that Goliath was a giant, but that he was a *yeti giant*? What's already a great story just got immeasurably better.

existing in the Bible. I would have assumed that at least one of the biblical authors would have given us a glimpse behind the dino curtain.

I mean, Solomon goes into wildly specific detail about sexy stuff and what to do if people are fighting over a baby (cut it in half, obvi)—so you're telling me he wouldn't have also thrown in some wisdom about dealing with a velociraptor posse that is harassing a major urban center? Or how to coax an obstinate stegosaurus into moving out of the road when you're trying to transport goods between cities? One of those just feels like something to mention, you know?

You might think this is a silly, simple thing to approach with such consideration. But when you're taking apart a piece of your foundational beliefs, it's never an easy procedure. It isn't just the thing itself you are removing; it's the emotional investment you've made in convincing yourself of its veracity. I'd held the idea that the Bible and dinosaurs were both incontrovertibly real, but I'd never actually worked out the timeline and the overlap until my late twenties. Once I did that though, it felt like the cat was out of the bag. I couldn't go back to a worldview where both triceratops and the tribes of Israel existed simultaneously. It just didn't square up.

But I wasn't done with these recalibrations. Five years later, at age thirty-two, I arrived at an even starker crossroads when my dad revealed to me that he'd been diagnosed with cancer.

I know paternal relationships can be rife with complexity. There can be emotional distance or physical distance or both. There can be complete and utter absence due to tragedy or absence due to a painful preference. I am one of the lucky ones. I have a great relationship with my dad. He was the best man at my wedding. He was the first person I hugged, weeping, after the birth of my first child. He is my best friend, the person I trust most in the world, and the person I most want to impress. His example and success as a parent is a ghost I will always chase.[2]

It was early November when I learned about the diagnosis. My parents had invited my sister and me to come over after church. The weather was brisk, but with a tinge of global warming; that is to say, it was one of those mornings where you needed a heavy jacket, but by lunch you risked melting into a heat coma if you hadn't layered. I wore a hoodie and shorts—a neat compromise that I thought would keep me cool outdoors but warm in my parents' house.

When I arrived at my parents', we didn't go inside. I don't remember why and I don't know if a reason was given. But I distinctly remember thinking that the fact that we were sitting outside was strange because there was no precedent for it in all my other visits to my parents' house. To this day, I don't know if my parents chose this to signal that something was amiss, or if they just wanted to be outside on a November day that had turned unexpectedly arid. Perhaps they knew this conversation was going to be sad and they didn't want to taint any room in the house with the kind of watermark of sadness that can seep into the walls from the conversation we were about to have. Regardless, I joined my mom, dad, and sister, and after some chitchat my dad cut to the chase.

"I have cancer," he said, very matter-of-factly, as though we were playing Go Fish.[3]

The cancer itself was multiple myeloma, which is a rare and

---

2. Not like a poltergeist or one of those fake malevolent ghosts from *Scooby-Doo*, more of an affable, benevolent ghost like Casper.

3. To be honest though, I don't know how to play Go Fish, so I don't know if you ever make straightforward declarative statements beyond "Go fish." If you don't, whatever; don't make a big deal about card games. There's nothing worse than people who take card games too seriously.

strange type of cancer. My dad was fifty-four at the time, which made it even stranger. My sister and I were urged to not google it, which is probably good advice for most any kind of information you dread. An expectation of hopefulness when you google information about sickness is like Bruce Willis trying to detonate a nuke on a moving asteroid: the most suicidal of suicide missions.

But we were given hope: there was a treatment plan. Also in our favor: they'd caught the cancer extremely early. My parents had been on a tour of Europe that followed notable landmarks of World War II. While there, my dad slipped in the shower, hurting his back. The pain never subsided, so when they returned home, he visited a doctor who identified the back issue, and, miraculously, evidence of the cancer.

I won't put too fine a point on my dad's diagnosis and treatment because that isn't really my story to tell, but I feel like I do have the margin to consider the strange and new ways it affected me— because there is nothing more millennial than making someone else's cancer about you. But similar to aligning my understanding of dinosaurs and the Bible, this experience did provoke a similar kind of reexamination that was less what I believed and more how I believed it.

When faced with something like a loved one getting cancer, it's not that it makes you doubt; I actually think it's quite the opposite. Enduring a trial or crisis like that holds a light to the foundation and structure of your faith, and like a lot of things, when given a stress test, you find the weak points. That's what I experienced: watching my mom and dad deal with his diagnosis shone a spotlight on everything in me that wasn't rooted in something substantial.

I may have had my trust issues with God early on, but I never doubted God's omnipotence. My belief in God as inherently good, all-powerful, and benevolent was pretty sturdy, but I'd never had to put this belief to the test. It was the spiritual legacy handed down to me, so why wouldn't I believe it? For my whole life, I generally understood that bad things sometimes happened in this world. And more specifically, I understood that bad things happened randomly.

I welcomed this arrangement. Emotionally, I had opted in and felt great about it. Until one of those randomly bad things happened to my dad. The cliché thing is to talk about how the immediacy of this pain exposed a sort of wobbly faith structure. And it definitely did that to an extent—but that's not the real exposé of what went on. My dad getting cancer didn't make me curse God, and it didn't make me reject everything I believed. It laid everything bare under the light of a previously unknown clarity.

I'm exceedingly fortunate in how, at thirty-two, this was the first margin call on my faith. I hadn't dealt with immediate death, tragedy, displacement, or anything else even vaguely traumatic. In this sense, I'd lived a very charmed life. But I'd also never been forced to hold a magnifying glass to my soul to see what would come up when times got tough. The unintended consequence of any trial is that it can clarify your purpose and resolve, and it can demand an accounting for why you believe what you believe.

Throughout this process, I never considered abandoning my faith. But it did provoke a remodel that I hadn't, up to this point, realized was necessary. This wasn't like a faith that needed some new counters, new paint, and better lighting—it was more like a full-on, let's-get-Chip-and-Joanna-in-here demo day.

To start with, I had a hard time with one seemingly stray detail: My dad falling in the shower was essentially the difference between life and death. Adding to that, my father is a coordinated, athletic, in-shape man. He's not a prat-falling machine like Chris Farley.

So the fact that he fell just as there was evidence of cancer in his body, but not so much that it had become fatally malignant, was an extraordinary needle to thread.

Which is why I've fixated on this origin story of cancer so much. For something that seemed so tinged with supernatural subtext, it seemed to beg a deeper consideration. During his treatment, on good days, I hoped that the early cancer detection was a tell of God's overall plan that he would be sparing my dad. On bad days, though, I worried about this being a viciously cruel hoax of hope where my dad would be taken from me so as to devastate me, leaving me vulnerable to some profound lesson I needed to be taught. As I alternated through these emotions, a more central subconscious question began taking root in my heart: Did God really run the world with that kind of tragic, Shakespearean aesthetic?

All the feelings were overwhelming, and it felt a bit like trying to disentangle the biggest mysteries about the nature of God. So I simplified things for myself and boiled it down to this: If I were to accept that bad things happen to good people, which I did, then it felt necessary to embrace a bitterly arbitrary randomness. Not godlessness or a reduction of his omnipotence, but rather acceptance that he lets the cancer chips fall where they may, so to speak.

Otherwise, if things *weren't* random, cancer happening to my dad couldn't intellectually hold up for me. Because while there is fear in randomness, there's also a certain kind of comfort in it too. Essentially, I was spiritualizing the bland idea "It is what it is" in contrast to the similarly bland idea "Everything happens for a reason."

But despite this reconstruction of my faith, I still couldn't quite square this with the revelation that my dad seemed to have been tipped off. If there was an overall governance of randomness, was his falling in the shower just a coincidence? As much as that neatly explained things, it also felt naive. But then the inverse was believing that God was using smoke and mirrors in the lives of us, his followers. And that didn't really feel right either.

I was down a different kind of road than I had gone down with the dinosaurs, but I was still unable to return to that simplicity that would have allowed me to accept it and move on. As I wrestled with this idea, I remember feeling like God was talking out of both sides of his mouth. And this made me very, very angry. With the cancer, sure, but also with God and the doublespeak I felt like he was always able to get away with.

Somehow this God, who supposedly knew everything and saw everything and could do anything, was able to get away with not really doing anything. I mean, I knew he sent his son, and that was a huge deal—the hugest of deals—but I was in a very "What have you done for me lately?" headspace. I felt inducted into a heritage of people who found themselves quietly resentful that God always got the benefit of the doubt for being vague and mysterious when really, it felt like he was disinterested. Otherwise, why not produce a miracle, sign, or wonder to help us with the anguish and fevered wonderings that accompany the pain native to our lives?

This problematic God character was endlessly frustrating to me, but as I examined that frustration, I realized that it wasn't God talking out of both sides of his mouth. *I was.*

As a writer, you have to develop a skill for characterization. Any fictional person you bring into existence, you have to give them a voice and a vibe. How do they talk? What's important to them? Are they one of those weirdos who eats pineapple on their pizza and brags about it or do they go pepperoni and double beef like a normal person? Whatever you do, you have to make a decision to articulate the person; otherwise, they get stuck in a purgatorial beigeness of existence. Why? Because they are your creation and you have to create them in your own kind of image or sensibility.

This is what I'd done to God. Even though I'd been taught that he had created me in his own image, my entire life was spent reducing him to mine. His ways, his thoughts, his decisions, everything from his grand unifying theory of everything to me getting a primo parking space to his purpose for why my dad got cancer.

Prior to my dad's diagnosis, I could reverse engineer everything God did so that it matched up to my perception of him. Whether it was dinosaurs and the Bible or why bad things are happening to your hero, I arrived at a logical understanding of God through a subconscious shape-shifting of who he was and what was important to him. This allowed me to maintain a sense of understanding and kinship with God and his supernatural mystery, while also feeling like I had a beat on why the supernatural Creator of all things everywhere of all time did the things he did. In a lot of ways, I analogized God to a Bill Belichick-led defense: rigid on fundamentals, but flexible on scheme. It felt like the perfect catchall to mind my foundational beliefs all while capturing the fluidity and mystery of who he was. I thought I had God pegged, but that was only because my understanding of him is what I'd faith-Frankensteined together.

After my dad walked us through his diagnosis and the treatment he would be embarking on, he related that he had first been given a preliminary diagnosis of lung cancer. This, considering his age and that particular kind of cancer's ruthlessness, would have basically been a death sentence.

It's strange what you remember in the critical moments of your life. Your brain widens out to note the strayest detail as though it's a forensic analyst at the scene of a crime. Every piece of information and reaction comes under scrutiny and is affixed on some mental corkboard of trauma. The poignant ones get permanent status and the superfluous ones are omitted and forgotten.

But a detail I'll never forget was my dad relaying that window of time when he was coping with the reality of what he thought was a lung cancer diagnosis. He told us that he remembered having bought white dress shirts earlier the day of his diagnosis, and, looking at them afterward, he realized that those might be the last white shirts he'd ever buy.

A few things about this anecdote.

- It quickly became superfluous given that his correct diagnosis was much more treatable.
- Anyone who knows my dad would know that even if he did have lung cancer, he'd have still bought more dress shirts. This is a man who mowed the yard in polo shirts and khaki pants. Like cancer was going to turn him into someone with the fashion sense of Artie Lange.
- This revelation of this anecdote remains acutely haunting to me, even now.

One of the great tragedies that many of us experience is the objectification of our parents. They can be avatars for so many things: authority, rebellion, oppression, love, respect, inspiration. But the one thing they rarely get to become to us is people. No matter how contorted the relationship, our parents always exist in a state of heightened symbolism. They aren't just people; they are totems for good and for bad and for a place where we aren't who we are now as much as who we were as kids. On some level, we're all aware of that and understand it to be true, but it's not a part of our active knowledge when we interact with them.

The idea that my dad underwent a dark night of the soul is irrevocably sad to me. Seeing him tethered to a kind of frailty and humanity that I'd rarely applied to him was jarring. Mostly, it was sad because, as his son, I knew that I could never be a party to helping him navigate that kind of dark night. And it made me sadder to know that there were entire worlds of his that I could never enter or understand. Yet another instance of two things being separately true: he is my father who exists uniquely to me, but also a person vulnerable to cancer and despair. Both of these things, however true they might be, refused to be balanced.

Dealing with the fear and worry about his cancer was a multidimensional issue. For one, there was fear for his health. What he would endure, and what if he didn't make it? Beyond that, there was a fear of the deeper stuff, like how to be. How to help. And then there was the wildly unmooring stuff like the fear of what his absence from my life and my family would bring. A child's life is always meant to be a torch of light in the darkness that extends beyond their parents' lives, passing the flame forward. I just wasn't ready for that torch yet. And even more immediate was the idea that I never would be. But I was confronted with something I didn't want to even consider. In a way, the definitiveness of death is almost a balm; because even if there was a microscopic chance of physical immortality, we would all cling to it like Jim Carrey clung to the potential of dating Lauren Holly in *Dumb and Dumber*—and we would still all be devastated when death invariably happened.

To deal with this fear, I returned to all the familiar hubs that had helped me formalize my identity. What better thing to do when in a crisis than to revisit the places that had helped me figure out my fundamentals? But sports felt like a distraction. My faith was in the middle of a sprawling rebuild. Even popular culture failed me. Do you know how many stories focus on dealing with loss? How many commercials deal with the fleetingness of time? Seemingly *all* the commercials. But I didn't want exposure to what I was dealing with; I wanted clarification on how to deal with it, and I wasn't getting it in any of the traditional places. For the first time ever, I was looking for definition in the untraditional, but to no avail. I wanted comfort and understanding, but all I was getting was fear and chaos.

I remember the day Stuart Scott, the *SportsCenter* anchor, lost his battle with cancer. It was a few months after I'd learned about my dad's diagnosis, and Ashley and I were driving to a Trader Joe's in Knoxville. On the way, we'd stopped at a McDonald's to get our kids some breakfast, and on the TVs inside the McDonald's I saw the news. It left me openly sobbing. Have you ever openly sobbed at a McDonald's? I would say it and Taco Bell are the two places least conducive to open sobbing.[4]

For so many months, it was just spinning wheels. I was fixating on not fixating on my dad, and not fixating on how I was succumbing to the most cliché of responses to crisis: the reconsideration of everything. The brutal reality I arrived at during all this was that my faith wasn't a faith; it was a curated worldview with a thin glaze of Christianity and a beaucoup of other priorities and qualities I wanted to be aligned with. Yes, I for sure knew Bible verses; and also yes, I'd taken the time to talk to strangers about my Lord and Savior Jesus Christ, but none of those things were authentically mine. They were all the vestigial remains of a learned ceremony. And even more,

---

4. Also, a foam pit at a trampoline park.

they were fossilized evidence of a sort of privilege that if unchecked can fool you into thinking a great many things, none of which are true, earned, or fully understood.

Throughout all this time, I prayed. I covered the entire evangelical spectrum:

1. On knees, hands folded, eyes closed, head bowed
2. Out loud in the car
3. In Bible studies
4. Email prayer chains

But even my praying was not an authentic gesture; it was a reflexive reaction to crisis. Still, it did plunge me into constant thoughtfulness about what I believed and what I was trying to understand about God. It was like a mindfulness on low heat, much different from the way I used to turn on the high heat of religion in bursts before turning it all the way off.

During this time I allowed myself to doubt. And not just soft-core doubts about dinosaurs or Jesus and alcoholic wine. I'm talking hardcore doubts about whether or not any of this is real. God, Jesus, the Bible, Ryan Gosling's vaguely New York-ish accent. Is all of this just an artful charade? Are we just in a simulation? Is the idea of God just a primitive impulse that evolved alongside us over millions of years? Or is he exactly and only what the Bible says? Or, is he something in between?

If I had to say where I arrived, I don't know that I could, because even now, I'm still processing my thoughts and feelings in a great many ways. I'm still trying to quantify and qualify and recognize what I believe and why I believe it. I know that may seem awfully anticlimactic or perhaps even cowardly to some, but I've had my fill of telling people the particulars of what they should think just because it's what I happened to think.

Also, if I'm being transparent, because I'm scared about reception. Like dinosaurs and God's role in a cancer diagnosis, there are a handful of things I hold in my heart that, while they feel true, also feel unable to coexist on the same spectrum of belief. I don't think this is rare, by the way. I think we all have to reconcile the things we've been told to carry with the things our hearts feel compelled to carry. And if that's you right now, I challenge you to let yourself wrestle with that juxtaposition and tension.

One of the Bible stories I genuinely loved as a kid was the story of Jacob wrestling God. The essence of the story is that Jacob wrestled God for several hours to a stalemate, until God dislocated Jacob's hip with a touch of his hand. I'm not Billy Graham, and I don't know what the original Hebrew of this passage suggests or how it informs the application we're supposed to take from it, but the thing that always spoke to me in this story was that God was fine with a little good-natured wrasslin'. Metaphorically and, evidently, literally.

Which leads me to this: as I worked through my dad's cancer (he's in remission, by the way), I found a space for myself between mindfulness and traditional evangelical praying. And it was there where I felt God speak to me, truly, for the first time ever. Not audibly, but loudly, vividly, and consistently in a voice that emanated from deep inside my heart. And in that voice, he reassured me that no matter what happened with my dad, God would always be bigger than I could conceive, yet more accessible than I could ever know.

He told me that I would find him in places I wasn't looking and in ways I wouldn't understand. After so many years of reverse engineering who he was, he gave me freedom from the burden of wondering in exactitude who he was and how he was.

He told me that there was room, so much room, for my doubt and my questions. That all of that was okay, because the God I had miscast into my narrative of a life and the God I'd misinterpreted and mischaracterized for all these years that was so into condemnation and rules and legality and guilt and shame—the real him was never about that.

And the churches and people who misappropriated his love as hatefulness in a charade of obedience? He told me their words came from the fraught authority and pretense that only conforming God to our own image can bring.

More than anything, God spoke to my heart and revealed that he really was fine with questions. Because at the end of the day, he knows that the answers to all the questions I'm wondering about, and have been wondering about for all these years, they've always led back to him. So why wouldn't they still?

Conclusion

On Conclusions

At the beginning of this book, I talked about how we underemphasize introductions. Now, here at the end, I wanna spend a brief second talking about how we put a hugely outsized importance on conclusions and goodbyes.

Clearly, this blame can be laid at the feet of Bruce Willis and Brad Pitt. *The Sixth Sense* and *Fight Club* both arrived in 1999 and set a generational notion in place, entitling pop culture consumers to the belief that conclusions and finales were immensely important. I'm pretty sure this is why as a society we're dealing with things like promposals, but I can't draw a direct line to that specifically. Yet.

Anyway, thanks to Ed Norton seeing an unreal Tyler Durden and Haley Joel Osment seeing unalive people, you're probably expecting me to tell you that I'm not actually Knox McCoy, a convivial weaver of anecdotes and pop culture elements into relatable ideas, but that I'm actually Keyser Söze. And that box you're holding? (*Quiet maniacal chuckle.*) Well, it actually has Gwyneth Paltrow's head in it.

JK. That was a total JK moment just then. I hope you weren't holding a box when you read that because that might have felt strange, and also because why are you holding a box and a book? Kick your shoes off and relax a bit, you know? I feel like it was Abraham Lincoln who said, "Life is too short to hold boxes and books while reading," and I have to say, that wisdom holds up in the modern era.

Anyway, do you know the worst part of this cultural evolution of conclusions? The unholy expectation springing forth from the loins of conclusions that they should also come with post-credits scenes. The intellectual brutality of this trend defeats me every time, even though I've lived through more post-credits scenes than I can count.

INT. MOVIE THEATER—EVENING

Knox and his stunningly beautiful wife, Ashley, sit quietly in a movie theater. The credits roll. Knox begins gathering his things and surreptitiously wiping all the stray popcorn off his shirt. Ashley remains seated.

ASHLEY

What are you doing?

KNOX

What do you mean what am I doing? The movie is over.

ASHLEY

But there's a post-credits scene.

> **KNOX**
>
> And?
>
> **ASHLEY**
>
> We have to stay for the post-credits scene.
>
> **KNOX**
>
> We extremely do not.
>
> **ASHLEY**
>
> You're going to sit through the whole entire movie but not watch the post-credits scene?
>
> **KNOX**
>
> Well, when you say it like that . . . still yes.
>
> **ASHLEY**
>
> Well, I'm staying. I want to see what it's about.
>
> **KNOX**
> (Pterodactyl screech of rage)

It's like wearing a hat on top of another hat, only the second hat is incredibly self-indulgent and it requires people to look at it. I need post-credits scenes like I need another white woman writing books telling me to live free and God hard.

But back to the larger issue of conclusions, I think the real trouble is that because we understand them to be the end of things, they take on a compressed amount of emotion and urgency only because our awareness of the end is heightened. We feel compelled to attach more meaning and influence to the end of things, when really the end is just an extension of everything you've already experienced.

Think of the *LOST* finale. That thing was like outrage catnip. It made people feel like they were taking crazy pills *and* their pets' heads were falling off all at the same time.[1] And this outrage was connected directly to the outsize expectations people had for it. What is the saying about expectations? That they are resentments waiting to happen? So true. And I think Abraham Lincoln said that too.

The problem people had with the *LOST* finale occurred because it was expected to be a transcendent experience, doubling as validation of their emotional investment through the answering of every single question and mystery still out there about the show.

And while I get that, I fully reject it as the trash opinion it is. That expectation dismisses all that time spent enjoying the mysteries, the flashbacks, and all the nicknames Sawyer made up for Hurley. To me, a good conclusion honors the spirit of what has been established.

Sonny Corleone went out in a violent hail of bullets, which is exactly how he lived his life.

---

1. Friends do let friends still make *Zoolander* and *Dumb and Dumber* references, FYI.

Quint from *Jaws* was eaten, which feels right given the obsession and hubris he had in relation to great whites.

Thelma and Louise die after driving their convertible into the Grand Canyon, which makes sense given the YOLO aesthetic informing most of their decisions.

The Nazi from *Raiders of the Lost Ark* got his face melted off, which feels supremely appropriate given that he was a godless piece of Nazi trash.

And I like this idea. Especially when you apply it to yourself. We are all careening toward any manner of conclusions: professional ones, emotional ones, and, yes, even physical ones. But however those things end, odds are they won't end with hugely provocative twists, but rather more in line with our journey along the way.

So back to my conclusion. I realize that throughout this book, I've been vulnerable. In some places more than I'd preferred, and in others less than I could have been. It is my hope that these moments communicate the idea that we're never closer to the heart of things than when we're willing to be vulnerable and transparent. That goes for God, who we are in relation to God, and how helpless we feel when trying to understand why Kevin didn't just call the cops in *Home Alone*.

So listen. With all that said, I'm not good at goodbyes. I tend to be more of a thinker than a feeler, and traditionally goodbyes involve a lot of feelings. So that's not something I really want to do here, even though the entire process of writing this book has been one large confrontation with my feelings. But I will say goodbye holding on to one feeling in particular: gratefulness.

I'm incredibly grateful, whether you purchased this book physically, digitally, or even if you're just leafing through it at a bookstore. All those options are exertions of effort, and to be honest, I'm appreciative of all of them. However you have come to find this page, I'm grateful that you've paid my words attention. It means more than you can ever know.

Practically, I'm a fan of the Irish goodbye (a.k.a. the introvert's goodbye) where you just leave. Some people think it's rude, but I think it's more about acknowledging the hope for a fluid relationship where there's not a need for a goodbye, since hopefully we can do this all again really soon. Because never forget what Abraham Lincoln said: "If you love a book reader, let them go. If it was true love, they'll come back and definitely read your next book." Good ole Abe. He really knew his stuff, didn't he?

Acknowledgments

First, I cannot say thank you enough to all the people who helped me put this book together. There are the people who helped me mold and shape this book into something actually readable, and then there are the ones who had very little to do with the actual writing process but so very much to do with everything that came before it. To all of you, you have my eternal gratitude.

No Thanks

No thanks to Chris Pine. Why are you so handsome? Settle down with your handsomeness. It's excessive.

No thanks to people who say things like "I don't even own a TV." Well, I do own one and guess what? It's awesome.

No thanks to the Oxford comma.

No thanks to Mr. L. from tenth-grade English who told me I was a terrible writer. I was, but you didn't have to say it in front of the whole class.

No thanks to Christian Brothers High School in Memphis, Tennessee. No one likes any of you and especially not your stupid baseball team.

No thanks to Jessie Spano. You can actually accomplish a lot on caffeine pills if you keep it together. This book is proof.

Thanks

Thanks to Vince Vaughn. Everything you do is magic. Even *True Detective* season 2.

Thanks to my youth minister, John Waters, for all your influence in the early formation of my faith. Ben Davis, you too, though I honestly have no idea what your title was. Vice youth minister? Assistant (to the) youth pastor? Whatever, you get the point.

Thanks to Chet LeSourd and John Lambert for teaching me how to write, how to read, and how to appreciate both.

Thanks to Paul Sausville for long talks about everything.

Thanks to Mark Davis for even longer talks about nothing.

Thanks to Eddie James, Tommy Woodard, and Brian Cates for teaching me about story, heart, and humor.

Specifically to this book . . .

Thanks to my editors—Megan Dobson, Meaghan Porter, and Sam O'Neal—for their immeasurable efforts in forming a mess of an idea into something marginally readable.

Thanks to the larger W Publishing group for buying into my vision for this book immediately and enthusiastically. (When someone sees your affinity for *90210* as a strength and not a weakness, that's lifelong partnership material.)

Thanks to my agent, Lisa Jackson, who looked beyond a very, very, *very* strange fiction proposal and saw a different kind of potential I wasn't confident enough to pursue.

Thanks to my partners at The Popcast Media Group, Jamie

Golden, Erin "The Edge" Moon, Jason Waterfalls, and Jordan Gordon Levitt for picking up my slack while I wrote this book. You all are the real MVPs.

Thanks to Laura, for being my initial guide through popular culture and who never flinched at letting me, her dopey younger brother, tag along everywhere she went.

Thanks, Mom and Dad, for your patience, encouragement, and unwavering support of me. Thank you for training me to love hard work and to appreciate a good sarcastic comment. Thank you for allowing a different kind of faith to emerge within me, and most of all, thank you for not making me go to Awana because you knew I hated Awana so hard.

Thanks to Rowe, Sidda Gray, and Marlowe. To borrow from the Avett Brothers, "Always remember there is nothing worth sharing like the love that lets us share our name."

Lastly, thanks to Ashley. You were the first to see the person I wanted to be all those years ago on AOL Instant Messenger. You lit the fire for all of this.

About the Author

Knox McCoy loves laughing and making people laugh. Really anything that's laughter-adjacent, he's into. He's also super into the word *swashbuckling*, and his dream is to one day use it in a bio.

Knox began podcasting in 2011 as a way to talk more about popular culture, and to his extreme surprise, he's still doing it every week on *The Popcast with Knox and Jamie*.

As a resident of the South, Knox's heritage is to enjoy football and barbecue, and he does so with great passion. He also enjoys zombie movies, police procedurals, and a good Netflix binge.

Knox lives with his wife and three kids in Birmingham, Alabama, where he works as a screenwriter and as the swashbuckling cofounder of The Popcast Media Group. (Dreams really can come true.)